The Ethical Marketer's Handbook for Mastering Affiliate Marketing

Comprehensive Step-By-Step Guide for Practical and Ethical Online Marketing

Steve Murry

© **Copyright 2023 - All rights reserved.**

The content contained within this book may not be reproduced, duplicated or transmitted without direct written permission from the author or the publisher.

Under no circumstances will any blame or legal responsibility be held against the publisher, or author, for any damages, reparation, or monetary loss due to the information contained within this book, either directly or indirectly.

Legal Notice:

This book is copyright protected. It is only for personal use. You cannot amend, distribute, sell, use, quote or paraphrase any part, or the content within this book, without the consent of the author or publisher.

Disclaimer Notice:

Please note the information contained within this document is for educational and entertainment purposes only. All effort has been executed to present accurate, up to date, reliable, complete information. No warranties of any kind are declared or implied. Readers acknowledge that the author is not engaged in the rendering of legal, financial, medical or professional advice. The content within this book has been derived from various sources. Please consult a licensed professional before attempting any techniques outlined in this book.

By reading this document, the reader agrees that under no circumstances is the author responsible for any losses, direct or indirect, that are incurred as a result of the use of the information contained within this document, including, but not limited to, errors, omissions, or inaccuracies.

Table of Contents

INTRODUCTION 1

CHAPTER 1: WHAT IS AFFILIATE MARKETING? 3

   WHAT IS AFFILIATE MARKETING? 3
      How Does It Work? 4
      Affiliate Marketing Types 5
   PROS AND CONS OF AFFILIATE MARKETING 6
      Pros 6
      Cons 7
      Breakdown Box 7
   UNDERSTANDING THE ECOSYSTEM OF AFFILIATE MARKETING 8
      The Ecosystem of Affiliate Marketing: Merchants, Affiliates, and Customers 8
      Building an Ecosystem 9
   EXPLORING DIFFERENT MODELS OF AFFILIATE PROGRAMS 10
   BREAKDOWN BOX 11

CHAPTER 2: INTERNET MARKETING 13

   WHAT IS INTERNET MARKETING? 13
      Reaching Potential Buyers Without Spending Too Much Money 14
      Building Your Authority 15
      Driving Traffic to Your Site 15
      Generating Leads to Your Links 15
      Driving Traffic to Your Affiliate Websites 15
   SEVEN INTERNET MARKETING STRATEGIES 16
      Search Engine Optimization (SEO) 16
      Content Marketing 17
      Social Media Marketing 18
      Influencer Marketing 18
      Pay-Per-Click Advertising 19
      Email Marketing 19
      Video Marketing 20
   GROWING YOUR BUSINESS WITH INTERNET MARKETING 20

CHAPTER 3: SELECTING A NICHE AND AFFILIATE PROGRAM 23

   SELECTING A NICHE 23
      Conclusion 26
   SELECTING THE RIGHT AFFILIATE PROGRAM 28

Finding Affiliate Programs 28
    Google 28
    Company Websites 28
    Directories 29
    Choosing an Affiliate Program 29
    What a Perfect Affiliate Program Looks Like 32

CHAPTER 4: BUILDING YOUR PLATFORM 33

Choosing a Domain Name 33
A Good User Experience (UX) 36
    Investing Time and Resources 39
Building a Successful Website 39

CHAPTER 5: BUILDING TRUST AND CREDIBILITY 43

Building an Ethical Affiliate Business 43
    Building Relationships 43
    Transparency About Commission 44
    Avoid Unethical Practices 44
    Authenticity Breeds Trust 44
    Addressing Negative Feedback 46
Facts and Statistics 47

CHAPTER 6: DRIVING TRAFFIC AND CONVERTING VISITORS 49

Driving Traffic to Your Website 49
    Quality Is Important 50
    Diversify Your Strategy 51
    Content Has Value 51
    Numbers Don't Lie 51
Search Engine Optimization (SEO) 52
    SEO Strategies and Techniques 53
    On-Page and Off-Page Strategies 55
    Implementing Technical Changes 55
    Higher Visibility Leads 56
Converting Visitors Into Buyers 56
Understanding Customer Psychology 57
Crafting Compelling CTAs 59
A/B Testing 61
Repeat 62

CHAPTER 7: ADVANCED AFFILIATE MARKETING STRATEGIES AND USING EMAIL MARKETING 63

Success Stories 64
Advanced Strategies 65
Email Marketing 67

The Ethics of Collecting Emails 68
SEGMENTATION FOR PERSONALIZATION 68
   Breakout Box 69
   Key Takeaways 70

CHAPTER 8: MONITORING PERFORMANCE AND SCALING YOUR BUSINESS 71

MONITORING PERFORMANCE 71
   Regular Strategy Updates 73
MAKING ADJUSTMENTS 75
   Achieving Optimal Results 75
   Being Proactive 75
SCALING YOUR BUSINESS 76

CHAPTER 9: LEGAL CONSIDERATIONS AND ETHICS 81

HONESTY ISN'T JUST MORALLY CORRECT 82
ETHICAL VALUES ISN'T A PREFERENCE 83
DEFINING ETHICS IN ONLINE BUSINESSES 84
   The Impact of Unethical Practices on Brand Reputation and Growth 84
   Understanding These Aspects 85
BENEFITS OF PRACTICING TRANSPARENCY AND HONESTY 86
TERMS OF SERVICE (TOS) AGREEMENTS 87
   Case Studies 88
PROFESSIONAL ASSISTANCE 88
SOUND KNOWLEDGE 91

CHAPTER 10: USING DIFFERENT PLATFORMS 93

BLOG 93
SOCIAL MEDIA 94
YOUTUBE 94
NICHE WEBSITE 95
PODCAST 96
EMAIL MARKETING 96
DIGITAL PRODUCTS 97
CONCLUSION 98

CHAPTER 11: MISTAKES TO AVOID 99

NOT HELPING, JUST SELLING 99
PRODUCING LOW-QUALITY CONTENT 100
IGNORING SITE SPEED 101
IGNORING READABILITY 101
NOT UNDERSTANDING THE PRODUCT YOU'RE SELLING 102
   Ignoring SEO 102
NOT UNDERSTANDING YOUR AUDIENCE 103
NOT DOING RESEARCH 103

- Not Building a Platform 104
- Choosing the Wrong Niche 104
- Writing Unprofitable Product Reviews 105
- Not Organizing Your Workflow 106
- Not Staying True to Yourself 106
- Getting Impatient 107

CHAPTER 12: CASE STUDY CORNER 109

- Ethics Can Make or Break Your Business 109
- Success Stories 111
  - *Darran Rowse* 111
  - *David McSweeny* 112
  - *This is Why I'm Broke* 112
  - *Chris Guthrie* 113
- Conclusion 114

CHAPTER 13: FINAL THOUGHTS 117

- The Future of Affiliate Marketing 117
  - *Predictions Based on Current Trends* 117
  - *Staying Ahead in a Rapidly Evolving Industry* 118
  - *Continuing Education Resources for Staying Up-to-Speed* 119
- Getting Started with Affiliate Marketing 120
- Final Thoughts 121
- Breakout Box 122

CONCLUSION 125

GLOSSARY 129

ABOUT THE AUTHOR 137

REFERENCES 139

Introduction

The growing reliance on affiliate marketing by online retailers signifies a shift in how products are sold today. —Journal of Marketing Research

Every great journey begins with a single step. And, as the legendary Chinese philosopher Loa Tzu once said, "The journey of a thousand miles begins with one step." Imagine yourself standing on the precipice of an incredible new adventure, ready to take that first decisive step toward financial independence and success. Welcome to the world of ethical affiliate marketing.

Picture this scenario for a moment: You're relaxing in your favorite armchair, sipping on a steaming cup of coffee (or hot chocolate if that's your thing), and watching the sunrise paint brilliant hues across the morning sky. Your laptop is open before you, silently displaying figures that make you smile, not because they're massive or groundbreaking (not yet anyway) but because they represent something more significant: Your hard work paying off through ethical means.

It sounds like a dream, I hear you say. Well, dear reader, it's time to wake up because this isn't just some sweet reverie conjured by an overactive imagination. It's real life, and it's within your grasp!

But shhh...! Not everyone knows about this well-kept secret. You see, there are ways to navigate online marketing waters without compromising our values or integrity, an art form we define as 'ethical affiliate marketing.

This book will guide you through these hushed whispers surrounding ethical affiliate marketing, unveiling its secrets like pulling back curtains on a sunlit window and revealing an awe-inspiring landscape beyond.

We will embark on a comprehensive exploration into the world of practical yet moral online business practices. We'll dive into what makes affiliate marketing tick and how you can create sustainable income ethically without resorting to cheap tricks or deceitful tactics.

Our journey will begin by defining "affiliate marketing" in all its glory, stripping away jargon until only simplicity remains, and translating complex terms into everyday language that even my grandmother would understand! We'll then explore strategies for building successful affiliate websites while maintaining high ethical standards. Lastly, we'll delve deep into how search engine optimization dovetails with ethical conduct to maximize profits without any feathers.

Imagine being able to create passive income streams while staying true to who you are, honoring not just yourself but also respecting those who visit your site seeking guidance or advice. Doesn't that sound wonderful?

Whether you're a new entrepreneur hungry for success or someone looking for an honest side hustle, buckle up! Prepare yourself for enlightenment sprinkled with humor and good taste as we delve deep into this amazing world together.

So here we are at the edge of our proverbial thousand-mile journey, teetering between excitement and trepidation as we look forward to unfamiliar terrain stretching out before us. Take heart, though, because together, we shall conquer each mile with grace and determination, one step at a time!

Ready? Let's take that first leap, and may our shared journey be filled with discovery, laughter, and, above all else, profit earned ethically.

Chapter 1:

What is Affiliate Marketing?

Affiliate marketing isn't something you can profit from overnight, it takes time, effort, and lots of learning to achieve great success. –Unknown

Imagine walking into a bustling marketplace. Traders are hawking their wares, customers are haggling and browsing, and you spot a unique opportunity amidst all this. You see an artisan selling beautiful handmade jewelry that's unlike anything else on the market. Intrigued, you strike up a conversation with the artisan and learn that he's struggling to attract customers despite his exceptional products.

You offer him a deal: You'll introduce his jewelry to your vast circle of friends and acquaintances if he agrees to give you a percentage of the profits from any sales generated through your referrals. The artisan agrees, seeing it as an opportunity to increase his reach without having to invest heavily in advertising or promotion.

This simple scenario encapsulates affiliate marketing: Promoting someone else's product or service in exchange for a commission on the sales made through your referral.

What Is Affiliate Marketing?

Affiliate marketing is when content creators sign up for programs with major brands to sell their products. Depending on the way the company pays its affiliates, there are various ways to earn. Some of these ways include pay-per-click, pay-per-sale, and through a set commission. Understanding and knowing which option is best will depend on you and your needs.

Affiliate marketing can benefit both the company and the affiliate because companies gain verified customers and get sales, whereas affiliates receive compensation for their hard work and marketing. Affiliates can create any type of content, from blog posts to YouTube videos and even TikTok videos. Some affiliate marketing programs require content creators to have a following of a minimum of 20, whereas others can require a following of upwards of 1,000 or more followers.

Besides the above, affiliate programs provide their affiliates with a unique link they should use when advertising products. This link makes it easier to track sales and compensate the correct affiliate. Even with most companies paying for sales they receive, you might also see companies willing to pay you for free-trial sign-ups, click on your link, and download a specific app.

Affiliate marketing can be done as a side hustle, but with the right strategies in place, you can also turn it into a full-time income source.

How Does It Work?

Companies or brands create affiliate programs for individuals to join so they can promote their products or services in exchange for compensation. The process of how affiliate marketing works is quite simple to understand if you remember the following points:

- The affiliate creates an ad for the brand.
- The customer clicks on the link.
- The customer makes a purchase.
- The brand records the purchase transaction.
- The purchase is finalized.
- The affiliate receives compensation.

With an entry-level affiliate program, you might be earning 5% per sale, whereas you might be earning upwards of 50% commission with high-end affiliate programs. You might even come across affiliate programs offering a set amount for every sale made.

Affiliate Marketing Types

> *Unattached affiliate marketing isn't a genuine business model, it's for people who just want to generate extra income.* —Elize Dopson

There are three different types of affiliate marketers, and understanding each of them will bring you one step closer to reaching the success you dream of.

Unattached affiliate marketing: This type of affiliate marketing is when the product you are advertising has no relation to the niche you are creating content in. This means you are just posting ads on your platform, and you hope someone will click on them so you can make a sale. This type of affiliate marketing often runs on pay-per-click campaigns.

It might be the easiest type of affiliate marketing because you will not have to do a lot of work to get started. You also don't need to build a reputation or trust with customers, which is perfect, especially if you don't have a lot of time on your hands.

Related affiliate marketing: This type is the opposite of the one above and means you sell products related to your niche. These affiliates often have an existing audience in their niche that is interested in buying the products they sell. This increases their trustworthiness and makes them the best source for selling certain products. Even if they don't personally use the products they advertise, their audience appreciates their recommendations.

The risk of advertising products you don't personally use is that you might not be aware if the product has high quality, and your audience might get disappointed. One bad review could lead to your whole audience losing trust in you, and this could hurt your affiliate marketing business.

Involved affiliate marketing: This type of marketing is when you recommend products you personally use and believe in. You believe the products you promote will change the lives of your audience. It might take a little longer since you need to build trust with your audience, but it could also mean higher profit margins if done properly.

Pros and Cons of Affiliate Marketing

Involved affiliate marketing is the way forward. It's rooted in trust and authenticity, which is best for your audience and business. –Elize Dobson.

You don't have to hide behind expensive PPC ads and hope for clicks and sales. An organic Instagram Story or blog post about your experience with a product will go a long way. –Elize Dobson.

There are various pros and cons related to affiliate marketing, and in order to succeed, you need to understand them all.

Pros

Easy to execute: All you would need to do to be successful in affiliate marketing is handle the marketing of the products you are affiliated with. Tasks like developing, supporting, and fulfilling orders are purely the responsibility of the brand or company.

Low risk: Joining affiliate programs is free of charge and if you have an established audience, you can start making money immediately. Affiliate marketing provides you with passive income, which makes it the perfect money-making machine.

Scalability: As your business grows, you are able to introduce more products to your audience while your existing products help you generate income without having to do extra work.

Even with all the pros of affiliate marketing, you should also take the cons into consideration before jumping in.

Cons

Needs patience: Your affiliate marketing business takes time to build and is not one of those get-rich-quick things. You might need to test out various platforms and strategies before you find the one that will work for you. You should also do research on the products you are looking to promote to ensure you know as much as possible so you can share your knowledge with your audience. You will also need to spend a significant amount of time creating blogs, social media content, virtual events, and other activities to help you generate leads.

Commission-based: Companies you are signed up with for their affiliate programs will not give you a paycheck every month; instead, they pay you per lead, click, or sale. This means that you would need to keep track of your content and encourage people to take action on your links if you want to make money.

No control: Each affiliate program has its own set of rules that affiliates need to abide by if they want to remain compliant. This means your competition should also follow the rules, which means you would need to create content that makes you unique.

Breakdown Box

Key Idea: At its core, affiliate marketing involves promoting others' products or services for commission on resulting sales made through one's referrals. It is a beneficial symbiosis between merchants seeking wider exposure and individuals or entities willing to leverage their online presence or audience base for monetary gains.

Now, let us address some misconceptions often associated with this field. Many view it as an easy way to make money online without much effort or investment; this couldn't be further from the truth! Successful affiliate marketers invest significant time and energy into building compelling content around promoted products and services while maintaining transparency with readers and viewers about the commercial relationships involved. This ethical approach builds trust, which ultimately fuels conversions and repeat business!

If things go wrong and your efforts aren't yielding the desired results despite doing everything right, consider seeking professional help. The world of digital marketing houses countless experts specializing in various niches, including SEO optimization and conversion rate improvement techniques aimed at boosting performance metrics critical within the realm of successful affiliate marketing operations!

Understanding the Ecosystem of Affiliate Marketing

Successful affiliate marketing is not about tricking people into buying a product, it's about making a genuine connection with them and solving their problems. –Pat Flynn

As the quote explains, it's important to build authentic relationships with your audience instead of lying to them about what you are offering. Understand and address the needs of your audience if you want to build loyalty and trust, which leads to success in the long term.

The Ecosystem of Affiliate Marketing: Merchants, Affiliates, and Customers

There are three key players in affiliate marketing, including:

1. **The Merchant:** This is the provider of the product or service being sold (the artisan). They create the affiliate program, establish the payment structures, and give out resources to help affiliates market their products and services.

2. **The Affiliate (also known as the publisher):** This is someone who promotes the merchant's products or services (you). As mentioned before, this could be in the form of websites, blogs, or other online platforms. Affiliates get paid when their audience performs an action that leads to the sale of a product or service.

3. **The Customer:** The person who buys the merchant's products or services based on the affiliate's recommendation. The way they react is a direct reflection of how successful the affiliate is with their marketing.

Affiliate marketing operates within a digital landscape where affiliates use their websites or social media platforms to promote merchants' offerings (David, 2023).

Building an Ecosystem

In order to create a successful ecosystem for your affiliate marketing business, you need to take the following into consideration:

Choose the right niche: Your business goals, audience, and market trends are the first considerations you have to keep in mind when choosing your niche. You need to establish what you are passionate about and work on that since this is your first step to building credibility.

Create a strategy: Define your business objectives and a marketing plan, including promotional tactics, audience identification, and your key performance indicators. As mentioned before, you need to evaluate your strategy regularly and make changes as and when needed to stay as competitive as possible.

Build relationships: You should not only build relationships with your customers and audience but also with the company you are affiliated with and other partners in your ecosystem. When you practice open communication, you build long-lasting partnerships and create mutual benefits for everyone.

Use SEO: Improving your SEO is a proven way to get recognized since it will help your search rankings and visibility. It will also get your content recognized and improve your long-tail keywords, which will help you attract traffic to your platform.

Monitor and analysis: There are various analytics tools available for you to use in order to keep track of your campaign performances. You should do this to determine whether you need to improve on some of your marketing strategies.

Exploring Different Models of Affiliate Programs

There are several models of affiliate programs available today (Sramek, 2023):

1. **Pay-Per-Sale:** The most common type where an affiliate can earn when a purchase happens through their referral link. This means that an affiliate will receive an established percentage of the sale their customer makes through their referral link. The commission percentage can be found in the affiliate agreement and is established by the company or brand. Pay-per-sale commissions range from 10% to 50%, depending on the product the affiliate is advertising.

   Pay-per-sale is an effective model offered to affiliates since it motivates affiliates to advertise products and convince their audience to make a sale, along with being one of the highest-paying models available in the affiliate world.

1. **Pay-Per-Click:** Affiliates get paid for every visitor they direct toward merchant sites. This is often seen as the model with the highest competition rate since it is the one most affiliates reach for. The best way to succeed with this model is to choose the right niche for your audience and convince them to choose you above the rest. In addition to this, pay-per-click affiliate models can further be categorized into the following:

   - **Pay-per-impression:** This is based on the impression your ads make on viewers and how they view them. These affiliates often have existing audiences, and their websites are niche-based.

- o **Pay-per-lead:** Affiliates using this model get paid for attracting visitors to the website of their affiliate program and filling in their information on the website. These affiliate programs can be found through financial services companies.

- o **Pay-per-action:** These affiliates get paid every time their audience takes action on their links.

1. **Pay-Per-Lead:** This involves getting rewarded for every lead generated, i.e., when visitors complete actions such as signing up for trials or newsletters on merchant sites via an affiliate link.

These different models provide flexibility, allowing affiliates to choose programs that best align with their audience engagement strategies.

Breakdown Box

To wrap up:

- Understanding roles within the ecosystem: merchants (product/service providers), affiliates (promoters), and customers (end buyers).

- Explore different program types suiting diverse engagement strategies: pay-per-sale, click-through, and lead.

- Remember, success lies beyond mere participation—it requires dedicated effort coupled with ethical practices focused on building genuine reader-viewer trust, leading to high conversion rates.

- Seeing professional help if needed—there's no shame in admitting defeat against the complex dynamics underlying modern internet-based businesses!

Remember, "It takes months to find a customer... a second to lose one." Vince Lombardi's wise words remind us that while attracting new customers might be exciting, the real game changer lies in retaining them; that's where true long-term value gets created!

Chapter 2:

Internet Marketing

In this chapter, I will be discussing what exactly internet marketing is, tips you can use to improve it, and some practical examples to help you see if your strategy is working.

It's not what you sell that matters as much as how you sell it. –Brian Halligan

Affiliate marketing overlaps with other internet marketing methods to some degree because affiliates often use regular advertising methods. –Shawn Collins

What Is Internet Marketing?

It's quite simple to understand what internet marketing is. In a nutshell, it is any marketing you are doing online to grow your business and get sales. There are various ways you can optimize your internet marketing and some of the channels you are able to use include:

- Organic searches

- Pay-per-click (PPC) ads

- Social media

- Online communities

- Email marketing

You can achieve this by creating captivating content and sharing it with your viewers on these channels to increase your reach. You are also able to show the value of your products, gain prospects' trust, and generate leads. It's worth mentioning that no channel is perfect and it would all depend on the group of individuals you are targeting and the social media channels they often visit.

Internet marketing can be an invaluable resource for your company for a few reasons, including:

- Reaching potential buyers without spending too much money
- Building your authority
- Driving traffic to your site
- Generating leads to your links
- Driving sales to your affiliate websites.

Let's look at each of these reasons in detail below:

Reaching Potential Buyers Without Spending Too Much Money

Almost six billion people around the world use the internet, which is more than half the population on earth. Internet marketing is used to increase the discoverability of your business without having to go through your budget a thousand times to see if you can afford it. Let's say you want to sell men's shoes to potential buyers. Then you will be happy to know that it gets searched for around one million times within 30 days all around the world.

If you find that your business is popping up in search results, then there is no doubt that it will continue to grow, and internet marketing helps with that. The key to Internet marketing is creating content buyers want to see. This will increase your visibility and encourage people to buy from you.

Building Your Authority

When using Internet marketing, you have the ability to let others see you as an expert in the brand you are promoting. The more your content adds value, the more reliable you will become to them. And to top it off, you are able to get attention and a market share. NerdWallet is the perfect example of this; they were able to establish their authority through internet marketing.

Driving Traffic to Your Site

Promoting your website along with internet marketing can help you increase the traffic you get on your website, especially when the content you create relates to your niche. When you get more traffic to your website, you can better connect with potential buyers and show them how the product you are selling will solve a problem they are facing. As this happens, you can turn simple viewing into action in the form of buying a product, downloading an eBook, reading additional articles, or signing up for a newsletter.

Generating Leads to Your Links

The idea behind using internet marketing for your affiliate business is to generate new leads who want to buy products from you. These leads are referred to as qualified leads. This means they are more likely to become customers who will look for your content because it may be relevant to them. The most effective lead-generation strategies are landing pages, emails, free trials, referrals, blogs, retargeting, ads, and social media.

Driving Traffic to Your Affiliate Websites

Internet marketing, when done right, will definitely help you sell more products. It allows you to use various channels to help customers find your products and see your pricing. For example, VTech promotes their products on social media, and people follow their account on

Instagram, which often leads them to buy products and see promotional posts when they go live. They also have a link in their bio, which makes it even easier for customers to access their website and make purchases of the products they are interested in. Doing this increases their opportunity to make sales and drive traffic to their website.

Let's look at some of the strategies you can use for internet marketing.

Seven Internet Marketing Strategies

There are various strategies available for you to use when attempting internet marketing, but I will be sharing the seven best ones with you below. Remember that the channels you use should complement each other. Never put all of your eggs in one basket, which means that you should not just focus on one channel to promote your products or services. So, do some research on your target audience and which channels they prefer to use in order to establish which ones you should be using.

Now let's look at those strategies:

Search Engine Optimization (SEO)

SEO is a strategy to help boost the visibility of your brand in search engines. This will increase the number of visitors that come to your site. Using the right keywords will help you with your SEO. For example, if you would like to get more traffic to your blog about pasta salad, then you might want to use "Make the best pasta salad" in your heading to come up in the top Google search results.

You will be able to outrank your competition when you answer buyers' questions and optimize your search, all while not spending more than your budget allows. The SEO strategy is not easy and takes time, effort, and resources, but it is possibly the most effective strategy over the long term. Your click-through rate will be estimated at around 27% if you can get your content to rank first in organic search results.

Look for topics your target audience would like to see when starting your SEO strategy; this means you would need to research keywords related to your products or services. You can do this by using a keyword search tool and then typing in a keyword closely related to what you are selling.

When you establish which keywords would work best, it's time to create the content your customers are looking for. In order to optimize your website, focus on on-page SEO and pay attention to your off-page SEO as well, this includes your backlinks and what you are posting on your social media channels.

Content Marketing

Content marketing is planning, creating, repurposing, and distributing relevant content that will help you drive sales and increase loyalty from potential customers. This will help you build your affiliate business and increase sales. An effective content marketing strategy helps you:

- Find your target audience
- Promotes the solution your product provides
- It tells you how to reach your customers

To build an effective content marketing strategy, you need to answer these questions:

1. Do you have people in mind for your content?
2. What unique solution do you offer?
3. Should readers choose your content over that of your competitors?
4. Will content marketing help you reach your goals?

5. Which content channels and formats will you use?

Every piece of content you produce should have a purpose, whether it be to educate your current audience or generate new business. Remember that content could include anything from videos to social media posts, eBooks, and studies and is not just bound to blog posts.

Once you have established what kind of content you want to produce, you should get organized. Find out how you will be publishing your content and do research on launching campaigns. You can create a marketing calendar for yourself to stay on track with when you will need to post your content.

Social Media Marketing

There are various social media platforms, including Facebook, Instagram, LinkedIn, and TikTok. You can grow a stronger bond with your audience when you regularly post content on these platforms. You can also grab the attention of new followers while trying to turn them into customers.

Social media is a great place to make people aware of your business hours and introduce them to seasonal products. You can also choose between organic social media marketing and paid social media marketing. Paid social media marketing will help you reach your objective, but organic marketing can be just as effective.

Social media marketing requires research, strategy, planning, creation, scheduling, and performance tracking to be as effective as possible. There are various tools available to help you with this so you can focus more on creating content and less on administration and scheduling.

Influencer Marketing

Influencer marketing is when businesses pay influencers to promote their products or services. If you want to grow your audience, then influencer marketing might be the way. When influencers advertise your products to their trusting audiences, they will be more likely to buy your product or even just visit your site.

Your first step in getting started with influencer marketing is choosing the right type of influencer to work with. When choosing a freelancer, you should look at their engagement rate instead of the number of followers they have. If you find that an influencer has a large number of followers but nobody is engaging with their content, then you might want to scroll past and look for someone else.

Pay-Per-Click Advertising

Pay-per-click ads are a strategy used to get people to click on their links and they pay a fee every time this happens. Google Ads is possibly the most popular option for this strategy and you can use Google search to find the best keywords to use for your advertisements.

When using PPC ads, you need to set your budget clearly, so you are not using everything to pay for running these ads. Before choosing to use PPC, do some research on the platforms your audience usually uses and then look for these campaigns there. Ensure that you do keyword research as well, and make sure to use them if you want to reach your target audience and receive a great yield from your efforts.

Email Marketing

Email marketing is used to keep customers up-to-date with special offers and as a way to get new customers through email. The first step to getting started with email marketing is building your email list. You can utilize lead-generation tools to assist you with this. You can also ask customers to sign up on your website using their email address in exchange for something like a downloadable template, webinar, video course, or e-book.

You can then categorize the emails you have received so you can personalize every email you send to suit the subscriber's needs. Categorizing emails allows you to:

- Get in contact with new subscribers

- Ask for reviews from your current customers

- Get feedback

- Get in contact with inactive subscribers

- Follow up on open orders

Always make sure the content you send is useful and compelling.

Video Marketing

The use of video marketing has seen an increase over the past few years, especially with the introduction of platforms like TikTok. Video marketing is very straightforward; it requires you to create video content that educates your customers and share it with them. You can choose to make short-form or long-form videos depending on the information you want to provide your audience with. Short-form videos are more relevant to platforms like TikTok since many people don't want to sit through longer videos to get the information they need anymore.

The algorithms that TikTok uses are meant to keep users on the app, so there is a higher chance for users to come across your content. You need to embrace authenticity if you want to be successful with video marketing on platforms like TikTok, but remember to have fun with it. Long-form videos are found on YouTube, and they are often used if you are looking to educate your viewers or teach them how to do something specific.

Growing Your Business With Internet Marketing

Internet marketing has revolutionized the way businesses reach potential customers. This is because of one reason: More people are spending time online than ever before. The best thing about Internet marketing is that you can get started without a big marketing budget and still reach potential customers. You can start by posting content on social media, redoing your existing content, and improving your SEO.

You can try out the various Internet marketing strategies for your affiliate marketing business to establish which one works best for you and brings in the most business.

As you can see, internet marketing has various benefits for your business, so you can try the different strategies I have given you or mix them up to suit your needs. In the next chapter, I will be discussing niche selection and how you can choose the perfect niche for your affiliate business.

Chapter 3:

Selecting a Niche and Affiliate Program

Choose a niche that aligns with your interests and passions.' — 'Riches in Niches: How to make it BIG in a small Market. –"Bullseye" by Susan Friedmann.

As you embark on your affiliate marketing journey, choosing your niche is one of the first and most critical decisions you'll face. This decision can make or break your success in this field.

Selecting a Niche

At its core, a niche is a specialized market segment for a particular kind of product or service. For instance, if the broader market is fitness equipment, a niche could be high-end home workout machines. The power of niches lies in their specificity; they allow you to target and connect with a unique group of customers who share common interests and needs.

In affiliate marketing, finding the right niche is like hitting the bullseye. It enables you to promote products that resonate with your audience, leading to higher conversion rates and profits. But how do you identify these profitable niches?

Your chosen niche should ideally align with your passion or expertise. This alignment makes it easier for you to create engaging content and adds authenticity to your promotions. For instance, if you're an avid gamer, promoting gaming gear would be more authentic than selling kitchen appliances.

Furthermore, profitability must be considered when selecting a niche. A quick way to gauge this is by researching potential affiliate programs within that niche. High-paying programs or those with high conversion rates are good indicators of a profitable niche.

The first and most important thing you need to take into consideration when choosing your niche is looking for programs you are passionate about. You need to love the products you are selling, or you won't want to continue working on them. The products you are looking to sell should also be sought after by your audience, or you might risk them losing interest.

You should also check the size of the niche you are interested in because if there isn't a demand for it, then visitors might not click on your links. If the niche has too much competition, then you might be competing against people who have been in the affiliate business for longer than you.

If you feel the product you are interested in is a specialized niche, then you can always incorporate other products into your business to attract more business. Take a look at your target audience and separate them by sex or age, and then see which products would resonate with them. You need to ensure that the niche you choose gives you the ability to create a successful business. That means that the niche should have various products related to it that people will be willing to pay money for.

It's also important for you to do research on your competition, but don't get discouraged if you find people already working in your niche. It's often a good sign since it means people are getting paid to promote those products. You will have a higher chance of making money this way.

Next up, do some keyword research on the products in your niche. Is there a specific problem your product can solve, or is there a question it can answer? Think of the top five answers so you can figure out if the niche will be profitable. Look for keywords that are easily accessible, and you can create content around them. These keywords should have low competition but should be searched regularly.

Keep the following in mind when choosing a niche for your affiliate marketing business:

1. **Do what you love**: If you can't find something you are truly passionate about, then you need to think about some of the things you have searched for over the past few months. Which phrases did you use, and what answers were you looking for? Were you able to answer the questions you had? The changes are so good that you can write between 20 and 30 posts based on the research you did.

2. **Are there affiliate products?** You might find it easier to start with Amazon and eBay affiliate programs, but you can also look at Clickbank, ShareASale, or Skimlinks. All of these affiliate programs can help you make money, and their sign-up is quick and easy.

3. **Look at the commission rate**: Do you need to have significant traffic in order to make money, and do the products offer a recurring subscription? You need to be willing to put in the work, so make sure you can do the math. If your conversion and click-through rate are both 10%, then that means you will be making $10 per sale. So you would need to have 10,000 clicks on your unique affiliate links if you wanted to make $1,000 a month.

4. **Look at the product range**: You need to have entry-level products if you want to make big sales. This means you would need to have more affordable products available on your platform if you want to turn visitors into buyers. People are often more willing to buy more affordable products first before they move on to more expensive products.

5. **Look at the competition**: Do a search for other affiliates making money with the same products. If they are, then you can too. A niche without competition might be a bad sign, so

you need to look for a niche with a healthy amount of competition if you want to be sure you will be making money.

Now let's delve into some key takeaways from this discussion:

1. Choosing the right niche is crucial in affiliate marketing.

2. Your chosen niche should align with your passion or expertise.

3. Profitability plays an important role in selecting a suitable niche.

Evidence supporting these statements comes from various case studies across different industries.

For example, let's consider Pat Flynn's Smart Passive Income Blog, one of the most successful platforms in affiliate marketing today. Flynn started his blog as an architecture exam guide before transitioning into digital entrepreneurship education. He was extremely passionate about both fields and he was well-versed in them.

Another example comes from "This is Why I'm Broke," an affiliate website featuring quirky products from around the internet. Clearly catering to an audience interested in unconventional items.

An inspirational quote perfectly encapsulates this topic from Steve Jobs: "People with passion can change the world." In our context, it means that combining passion with strategic choices (like choosing the right profit-making niches) can transform ordinary marketers into successful ones!

Analyzing these examples reveals that successful affiliates chose niches where they had interest and expertise while ensuring profitability was viable.

Conclusion

Successful affiliates choose their niches strategically based on interest, expertise, and profitability potential.

Here are some interesting bullet points highlighting essential considerations when choosing a profitable niche:

- Identify what interests, passions, and expertise areas you possess.

- Research existing affiliate programs within those areas.

- Evaluate the potential earnings and conversion rates associated with each program.

Identifying passions, interests, and expertise areas coupled with diligent research aids in selecting profitable niches.

Leveraging data further highlights why choosing the correct niches matters so much. According to Statista Data (2017), over 35% of affiliates reported earning more than $20k annually by focusing on specific lucrative niches!

To start identifying profitable niches:

1. List down all possible areas that match your interests, passion, or expertise

2. Use keyword search tools (like Google Keyword Planner or SEMRush)

3. Look out for keywords with decent search volumes but lower competition

4. Research existing affiliate programs under these keywords

5. Evaluate each program's commission structure and payout frequency

6. Choosing those that match the best against profitability criteria

Remember! Success doesn't happen overnight! It takes time and patience; however, armed with the right knowledge about how pivotal 'niche selection' impacts overall performance, you're closer to achieving the desired success! Good luck!

Selecting the Right Affiliate Program

You might get overwhelmed with the idea of an affiliate program, but with the tips and tricks you will find in this chapter, it will get a lot easier from here on out. So let's get started.

Finding Affiliate Programs

There are a lot of ways you can go in search of affiliate programs, but some of them can be daunting and very time-consuming. I would like to give you some of the best ways to search for legit and profitable affiliate programs so you can start making money immediately.

Google

The simplest and most straightforward way of finding affiliate programs is by using Google search. You can type affiliate marketing programs along with your niche into the search bar and you will find all the companies offering programs for their products. Be sure to check what various companies call their affiliate programs. Spotify calls their program the partner program, and Amazon calls it their associate program. Be sure to check if you can live anywhere in the world before applying to an affiliate program, since various companies have strict regulations against working with individuals from other countries.

Company Websites

If you have a specific company in mind, then you can go ahead and look at the company's website to see if they offer an affiliate program. You can scroll to the bottom of the web page to see if they have a link to an affiliate program, since this is where most companies hide theirs. You will also find detailed information on what the program offers, including the terms and conditions related to working for the company.

Directories

You can go in search of affiliate program directories when looking for the perfect affiliate program. These websites help you compare various programs, which cuts down on your research time and streamlines your application process.

Choosing an Affiliate Program

We all want to make money while we sleep, but finding the right way to do it can be tricky. Even though affiliate marketing is highly profitable, it's important to choose the right programs for you if you want to be successful. Below are a few considerations you need to keep in mind when choosing an affiliate program that will suit your needs.

You shouldn't just pick the first affiliate program you come across because you might not see the results you want. Ask yourself the following questions when looking at affiliate programs:

What is the market reputation of the program? Looking at the market reputation of an affiliate program is the best way to see if the company is legit. Always look at the credibility of the company and find reviews from previous and current affiliates to establish what they think. Ensure to check their engagement rates on social media, as it will give you a good indication of what people actually think about the business and their products.

Brand names are not always the most important consideration when choosing an affiliate program. You should also check the product quality in order to keep your audience happy. Ensuring product quality meets high standards will increase your chances of building lasting affiliate relationships. This improves your reputation and if you build a successful strategy, you can build a successful business for yourself. Your reputation could be damaged if you successfully market a poor-quality product.

Is the product in your niche? You can sell anything you want, but the fact is that focusing your time and energy on niche-specific programs would give you better results. This means that if you have a website or blog surrounding the sport, then you should look for affiliate programs that allow you to promote sports equipment. This makes your website a one-stop shop for all your audience's needs.

Remember, your audience might get frustrated if you advertise products that are not relevant to them. If you do find a product that doesn't relate to your niche but that you think might be profitable, then look for ways to include it in your content.

What is the conversion rate of the program? Profit is possibly the biggest reason for you to get into affiliate marketing. It works on a cost-per-sale basis, so you should choose a program that has a high conversion rate in order to get sales and make a profit. When looking at conversion rates, it's best to find programs that pay at a rate per sale or percentage-based commission, since these are the most popular amongst affiliate marketers.

Is the niche saturated? The returns you get on the product you want to market might be very low if there is too much existing competition. You can use competition metric tools to check your competition before applying. Look for products with less competition if you want to make a decent amount of profit.

Can you get tools and resources? You need to look for affiliate programs that understand the need to create promotional campaigns and that make it smooth for affiliates to do so. Affiliate programs that support their affiliates on their marketing journey will provide them with banner ads, email templates, demographic data, client testimonials, and creatives so they can focus on other advertising. These affiliate programs will help you make the most of your affiliate marketing journey.

Sales tracking system: Ensure that the affiliate program you choose to join has a system in place to track your sales. Having this system in place will help you keep track of the impact you are making and if you are having a dip in the marketing strategies you are using. You can use the data you gather to analyze whether you should consider another strategy or modify the one you currently have.

What is the cookie life? The cookie life is the period in which you are able to receive a commission for each click you bring to an affiliate program. This all means that if customers click on the link after your time has passed, then you won't be receiving commission from that click. You should always look out for affiliate programs with longer cookie lives.

What are the terms and conditions? Before joining an affiliate program, always make sure to read the terms and conditions thoroughly. If you miss a key section in the terms and conditions, you might find yourself in hot water. Some of these terms include the restriction of certain traffic channels. This means you could lose income from a client who clicks on your link from one of these channels.

Choose known or used products: Choosing an affiliate program from a company that sells products or services you use and trust is always a good way of building your business. You will already have the necessary product knowledge to successfully market it to potential customers, giving you an advantage in the industry. You will also be able to see if your customers will be interested in your chosen product.

However, this should not be your selling point. If you believe a product has value, then learn as much as you can about the product before you start promoting it. Do some research on previous customer experiences to determine whether the product is a good fit for you.

As you can see, there are many considerations when choosing the right affiliate program for your needs. It also takes time and research to ensure you are signing up for something that is not just profitable but also aligns with your niche.

Traffic Leaks: Traffic leaks are links that take customers to other sites. This means you can lose commission because the customer did not make a purchase on your link but instead on a link that was attached to yours. Affiliate programs often fail as a result of traffic leaks, and this is why it is so important to check for them.

What a Perfect Affiliate Program Looks Like

You might struggle to find the perfect affiliate program for your niche, especially when you choose one that isn't widely known to others. A perfect affiliate program should contain the following:

- Popular or high-quality products, or both
- High commissions or recurring commissions
- Extended cookie lifetimes
- Easy-to-understand terms and conditions
- Has a welcoming environment
- I can help you track your performance

Considering all these things when searching for an affiliate program will ensure that your business will flourish and make significant profits.

Chapter 4:

Building Your Platform

Your website should be your calling card or your business front porch. –James Schramko

The world of affiliate marketing is not just dynamic but also filled with opportunities. An essential component of this journey is the website or digital storefront. Just as a physical store needs to be appealing and functional, so does your virtual one. The process of creating such a space might seem intimidating initially but rest assured, it's simpler than you think.

In my experience in the field of affiliate marketing, I've come across many websites that failed to make an impression or missed out on potential conversions due to simple oversights. A major part of this oversight often lies in choosing the right domain name that truly reflects your brand. A catchy domain name makes your website easily memorable and significantly impacts how search engines perceive it.

Your website isn't just about appearance; it's about functionality and user experience (UX). Every element should serve the purpose of converting visitors into customers. This includes clear navigation menus, high-quality images and videos showcasing products or services, compelling call-to-action buttons, and much more.

Choosing a Domain Name

Key Takeaway: Your domain name should reflect your brand identity while being easy to remember and unique.

Now, let's take a look at some evidence supporting our points above. According to data from Virisign Inc., as of 2019, there were over 350 million registered domain names globally, indicating tough competition for attention online.

Let me give you an example: Back in 2007, when entrepreneur Andrew Wilkinson started his software design company Metalab, he chose the domain Metalabdesign.com, which was long and difficult for people to remember accurately. After struggling with this issue for years, they finally changed their domain to "meta.xyz," which was short, meaningful, and easy to recall, resulting in increased traffic on their website instantly.

As Steve Jobs once said, "Design is not just what it looks like and feels like. Design is how it works." This quote speaks volumes about why UX matters significantly when building an affiliate marketing website.

Let's take a deeper look into how you can choose the right domain name for your affiliate marketing business:

1. Keep your name short: This tip might seem a little obvious, but long domain names might be more difficult to remember and users might not be able to insert them into their URL bar. If your domain name is difficult to remember, then you might not be able to build a relationship with your audience.

2. Think about pronouncing it: Make your domain name as straightforward as possible. Avoid using slang, hip-hop language, or localized language or slang. Avoid using words that can only be known in the country you are living in. Your audience might come from all over the world and this could prevent them from choosing your platform.

3. Make it unique and easy to brand: Your domain name should not just be easy to remember, but it should be unique enough to stay in your audience's mind. If your domain name is too long, then your audience might not think it's unique, and you will have a harder time selling it.

4. Choosing the right domain extension: The most common domain extensions are ".com," ".net," ".org," ".co," and ".us." The most trusted domain extension to date is still ".com," so it is still the one I would recommend. If a ".com" extension is not available for your website, then you might want to consider using ".org" or ".net."

5. Think ahead: As your affiliate marketing business grows, you might want to move into various other niches to increase your profits. Because of this, you don't want to restrict yourself by choosing a niche-specific domain name. You need to think ahead when choosing your domain name.

So, to recap the information above:

- Keep your domain short and sweet
- Have it easy to pronounce
- Make it unique and easy to brand
- Choose the right extension
- Consider the future.

Consider these real-life cases: In 2012, Google redesigned its YouTube homepage, focusing on simplicity and increasing page views by 6% overnight! Similarly, eBay improved their checkout processes, reducing steps from seven to three, ultimately increasing sales by $300 million annually!

Remember that creating a platform and choosing the right domain name is nearly impossible because you might end up thinking you should have chosen another one a year from now. But stop overthinking it and just get it going.

A Good User Experience (UX)

Some interesting bullet points:

- As per Adobe, companies with highly effective UX have higher stock performance.

- Econsultancy found that for every $1 invested in UX, results can bring a $100 return!

- A study by Forrester reveals mobile sites with superior UX convert up to three times more than those without!

When you create your platform, you need to keep the user in mind. This will allow you to increase your user experience and help you build your affiliate website. The user experience you create starts with information about the product you are selling and ends with the customer service you provide.

The user experience has to do with delivering meaningful and relevant products to your audience while achieving your business goals. The platform you create for your affiliate business should be both helpful and engaging. This helps you build loyalty, attract new customers, and increase your profit. Another advantage of having a great UX is that you will be able to stand out from your competitors.

On the other hand, if you don't keep user experience in mind when creating your platform, you might risk leaks, which can hurt both your business and the product you are selling. You might also end up with frustrated customers, a higher bounce rate, lower conversions, and a reduction in profits.

Below are eight steps you can take to improve your platform user experience:

- Increase white space: This is often an overlooked point since many affiliates want to fill their platforms with information, but when you add enough white space, you allow your website to breathe and it will look refined. You might need to do some research about what is needed and what you should tell your customers about your platform.

- Increase your CTA visibility: Take the visual effect of your website into consideration when creating your platform. Humans rely on this to help them make purchasing decisions. Create tabs like 'Shop Now' or 'Sign Up' to help visitors on your website take action. It also helps customers know what they need to do because they will see these tabs clearly. Experiment with different colors on your website and what they represent. The colors you choose to use might send five different messages to visitors, so consider running an A/B test to get the best colors for your website.

- Improve your loading speed: Customers don't want to waste time on websites that take too long to load. They will be more likely to click out and look for another site if they are unable to get the information they need when they need it. Ensure you modify your images, websites, and interactions before adding them to your platform. If these components are more compact, it will help increase the loading speed of your website.

- Increase intuitive navigation: Carefully construct the website's architecture and navigational tabs so users can easily see where they are and where to go to find the information they need. Some of the things you need to remember include:

    o Brand logo: Your logo should be a link to your website homepage so users can easily find their way back.

    o Headings: The headings you add to your platform should stand out from the rest of your content.

    o Breadcrumb navigation: This can be used to link important information on your platform. It will also help readers look at various content to get the most out of your platform.

- UX research: Do some research about what customers want to see on your website so you can give them what they want.

- Add the following main categories to your homepage: Your homepage is the window to the rest of your platform. If customers are not intrigued by this, they might look for another website. To improve your homepage, you need to think about the words and images you use. Remove useless information, give information about your products, and address any pain points your customers might have. Add the most important product features and solutions they offer to the homepage along with a link so customers can easily find your purchase link.

- Test usability: Always look for areas for improvement on your platform. This will help you improve your customer interactions and remove friction points. It will also help you streamline the completion of specific tasks customers have to do. There are various tools you can use to help you with this without having to go through tons of data yourself.

- Utilize product images: When creating your platform, avoid using generic stock images. Your audience would have already seen these images on another site and this could make your platform inconsistent. Negative feelings are difficult to shake off, so you need to prevent your audience from developing them. Use as much promotional material and real product pictures as possible if you want to build trust and help your audience become loyal.

- Make it mobile-friendly: More and more people prefer to use their mobile phones to search for information, so you would need to ensure your customers are able to reach your site by using their mobile phones. Google has started penalizing websites that are not catering to both search engines and mobile devices.

Investing Time and Resources

You may be wondering how I apply all these insights to building my successful affiliate marketing site. Here are some specific action steps:

1. Choose Domain Name wisely: Keep it short and memorable, relating closely to your business.

2. Make Navigation Intuitive: Group related items together under clear headings.

3. Use Quality Images and Videos: High-resolution media adds credibility and trustworthiness.

4. Include Clear CTAs: Guide users towards desired actions, e.g., "Buy Now," "Sign Up."

5. Optimize Load Speeds: Slow sites frustrate users, causing them to leave prematurely.

Building a Successful Website

Building successful websites involves careful planning around key aspects like Domain Names, Navigation, Media Content, Page Speeds, etc.

You can follow the easy steps provided below to ensure your affiliate marketing platform will be successful.

Choose your niche: This topic was discussed earlier in this book, but I would like to remind you of the importance of choosing your niche again.

Choose your website type: Choosing your website type is another important thing to consider if you want to be successful with your affiliate marketing business. Some of the most popular website types include:

- Blog: Individuals who own blogs often create content and then incorporate affiliate links into the content. If you choose this website type, then you need to be careful of the links you add because you don't want the website to come across as an affiliate site.

- Retail listings: This website type often looks similar to other eCommerce websites, with one difference. The products advertised on these sites are actually links to the company that sells them (this is similar to drop shipping).

- Review sites: These affiliates often test the products they recommend to their audience so they can be sure the products they advertise are of high quality. When choosing this website type, you also have the freedom to ask others to review the same products.

- Comparison sites: As the name suggests, when you own this type of website, you search for the same product at various stores and then help your audience purchase from the most affordable one. You can add your affiliate links here, as well as reviews from users.

- Deals sites: These sites offer their audiences daily deals from various companies and manufacturers. You are also able to give your clients coupons you receive from these websites.

Choosing a domain name: This tip was also covered previously, and once again, I would just like to remind you of the importance of choosing the right domain name.

Choose your web hosting services: Another important part of creating your platform is choosing a web hosting service that works for you. Choose a web hosting service that has high quality and will serve you over the long term. Keep the following in mind when making your choice:

- Speed: Look for a web host who can provide you with a stable and fast server so your audience won't have to wait for your site to load.

40

- Security: You need to check if your web host will provide you with an SSL certificate and backup services that will help protect you against malware attacks.

- User-friendliness: Setting up your webpage should not be too time-consuming, so look for a web host that gives you a control panel that will help you.

- Price: Obviously, this is one of the most important things to consider when choosing a web host because you don't want to break the bank when you are just starting out. Prices for web hosting can range from $2 to $50, depending on the type of website you want to create.

- Support: You never know what will happen and you need to know that someone will be there to help you through any obstacles you might face with your site.

- Scalability: As your website grows, you might want to upgrade your web hosting plan. Ensure your web host offers this.

Share links: Once you have your platform or website all setup, it's time to start sharing your affiliate links. You can do this using two methods:

- Email marketing: Collecting emails and sending customized affiliate offers to your audience is possibly one of the most effective marketing tools you can have. You can incorporate a tool like Mailchimp or SendinBlue into your website to help you manage your subscribers, track your performance, and create emails.

- Social media: Social media continues to be the best marketing tool you can have to share both your platform information and your affiliate links. You can utilize Facebook, Instagram, and even TikTok to promote your business. Avoid creating content that sounds like a sales pitch, and add hashtags relevant to your content.

A well-designed site will guide visitors seamlessly through its pages, leading them directly toward conversion points without any confusion or distractions along the way. For instance, Shopify uses minimalistic designs with clear CTAs that guide users effortlessly through their buying journey.

After reading this chapter, you feel inspired and energized to tackle tasks ahead with full confidence, knowing each step taken today will contribute towards building profitable digital storefronts tomorrow!

Chapter 5:

Building Trust and Credibility

It takes 20 years to build a reputation and five minutes to ruin it. If you think about that, you'll do things differently. –Warren Buffet

Welcome to the intriguing world of ethical affiliate marketing. You're about to embark on an enlightening journey that will arm you with knowledge, strategies, and actionable insights. This chapter is about a critical aspect of your career as an affiliate marketer: Maintaining trust with customers while promoting products.

In the realm of affiliate marketing, it's not just about selling; it's also about building relationships. Over time, I've realized how crucial this facet is. When you recommend a product or service, your audience trusts your word. They buy not only because they need the product but also because they trust you.

Now let's delve deeper into this fascinating topic.

Building an Ethical Affiliate Business

Building Relationships

The first thing you need to do when starting an affiliate marketing business is build relationships with affiliate partners who share the same values as you. This will also help you build a relationship with your audience because you will have a verified partner on your side.

Transparency About Commission

The next important point is transparency about commissions. Honesty is always the best policy here; there's nothing wrong with earning from one's recommendations, provided one does so ethically and openly. Your audience deserves to know if you benefit financially from their purchase using your link.

In the world of affiliate marketing, marketing transparency has a few important roles to play. You need to tell your audience who you are affiliated with through clear disclosures, and you need to show where you add affiliate links in your content. This will help you take challenges head-on and build individual customer service. Be as clear as possible about the commission you are earning through all marketing strategies to ensure full transparency.

Avoid Unethical Practices

Tasks like click spamming, data selling, and URL hijacking are all considered unethical methods of affiliate marketing. It could harm the way your audience sees you and your credibility. Always follow the guidelines set out by the industry and ensure you remain compliant by using various tools and resources.

Affiliate marketing continues to increase with more and more people starting their businesses, which means that new consumer privacy laws are being put into place. Reviewing these laws is of utmost importance if you want to continue to remain compliant in the industry and not run into any trouble with your audience.

Authenticity Breeds Trust

Promoting products we truly believe in is fundamental for ethical affiliate marketing. It ensures authenticity and credibility when we communicate with our audience. It's akin to recommending a good book to a friend or suggesting a favorite restaurant. It comes from personal experience and genuine belief in its worthiness.

Always promote what you genuinely believe in and be transparent about commissions earned.

To back up these points, consider research conducted by Drs. Matthias Sorberg Winkler and Tobias Schlager at HEC Lausanne University on consumer behavior toward online influencers' sponsored content (Winkler & Schlager, 2020). Their findings suggest that consumers place a high value on authenticity—they respond more positively to endorsements perceived as sincere than to paid promotions hidden under the guise of spontaneous content.

For example, Sarah has been blogging about eco-friendly lifestyle choices for three years. She promotes only those brands she believes align with her values around sustainability, and she does so transparently by disclosing her commission earnings each month on her blog. This practice is appreciated by her followers, who find her approach honest and trustworthy.

As Eleanor Roosevelt once said, "People grow through experience if they meet life honestly and courageously." This quote rings true even today, especially when applied to our context of maintaining consumer trust within affiliate marketing dynamics.

Analyzing these further reveals that trust needs nurturing over time; it isn't something built overnight or maintained effortlessly; it requires consistency in actions aligned with stated values and clear communication channels where any concerns can be addressed promptly and respectfully.

On examining case studies related to ethical affiliate marketing practices within e-commerce platforms such as the Amazon Associates Program or ClickBank Marketplace, both popular choices among marketers, one discovers numerous examples where marketers have successfully built lucrative careers while maintaining high levels of consumer trust through consistent adherence to principles discussed earlier, promoting genuine belief-based products and services along with full disclosure regarding commission earnings.

Addressing Negative Feedback

Promptly and effectively addressing negative feedback goes a long way toward reinforcing consumer trust. Feedback is extremely important when you run an affiliate program because it will help you improve all aspects of your business. You should avoid having negative feedback cloud your judgment, as this could negatively impact your business.

Here are some interesting bullet points encapsulating noteworthy aspects:

- Consumers appreciate honesty. Transparency regarding financial gains enhances credibility.

- Swift responds and takes action to address negative feedback, strengthening customer loyalty.

- Always say thank you for the feedback, whether it's positive or negative. You need to take the time to show your audience you appreciate them and their opinion, as this will help you improve the service you are offering them.

- Take note of the feedback you receive so you can take immediate action. Take the time to see what your audience thinks about the content you are providing them with so you can change it up if they don't like it.

- Request more details on the feedback you receive. The more detail you can get about the feedback you receive, the more enabled you will be to make the necessary changes your audience wants to see.

- Offer to fix things. Receiving negative feedback is never pleasant, but it's how you respond to it that really matters. You need to be willing to turn a negative experience into a positive one if you want to be successful.

However, like any other business venture, negative feedback can sometimes occur concerning recommended products or services—even if we wholeheartedly believed in them when recommending them.

Facts and Statistics

The third key takeaway revolves around facts and statistics highlighting trends within the ethical affiliate marketing industry:

- According to Statista Data (2021), approximately 81% of customers rely on friends or family recommendations before making purchasing decisions, indicating the importance placed upon trusted referrals.

- A Nielson Global Online Consumer Survey report indicated that consumers worldwide are most likely to trust word-of-mouth advice from people they know (Nielsen, 2009).

Statistical evidence underscores the importance of building and maintaining consumer trust for success in affiliate marketing.

As per an insightful research paper published at Harvard Business School titled *Do Friends Let Friends Buy Socially Irresponsible Products?* The authors found that individuals were significantly less likely to endorse products that conflicted with their social responsibility norms, underscoring the importance placed upon alignment between personal beliefs and values and the product or service being promoted (Hildebrand et al., 2017).

So how do we navigate this terrain? Here are a few steps:

1. Know Your Product or Service Well: Before promoting it, understand its features and beliefs.

2. Be Transparent About Commissions: Clearly disclose any financial benefits received from purchases made via referral links.

3. Handle Negative Feedback Constructively: Respond quickly and empathetically, addressing concerns raised and ensuring remedial steps wherever feasible.

4. Constant Learning/Evolution: Stay updated about the latest industry trends, ensuring relevance and effective promotional strategies are being used.

Affiliate marketing isn't merely transactional; it involves building relationships based on mutual respect and honesty, paving the path to a sustainable, successful career therein!

Chapter 6:

Driving Traffic and Converting Visitors

Your website is the window of your business. Keep it fresh, keep it exciting. –Jay Conrad Levinson

In the affiliate marketing world, traffic is your business's lifeblood. It's not just about having a website; it's about getting people to visit that website. The more traffic you have, the higher your chances of earning commissions from your affiliate links. So, let's talk about how you can drive more traffic to your site.

Driving Traffic to Your Website

The key to driving traffic lies in understanding where these visitors are coming from and optimizing those channels. A common misconception amongst beginners is that all traffic sources are created equal, but this couldn't be further from the truth. Some sources provide higher-quality visitors who are more likely to convert into sales or leads than others.

For instance, organic search engine traffic tends to be highly targeted because these users are actively searching for information or solutions related to what you're offering. This makes them prime candidates for conversions if you can deliver on their needs.

On the contrary, social media platforms may offer high volumes of users, but they might not always be in a purchasing mindset when browsing through their feeds. That doesn't mean they're worthless—quite the contrary! With carefully crafted content tailored toward user behavior on each platform, social media can become a significant source of quality traffic.

Quality Is Important

It's not about quantity when it comes to driving website traffic; instead, focus on quality and relevance.

Paid advertising channels also present an opportunity to attract targeted visitors quickly—provided you're willing and able to invest some money upfront. Google AdWords and Facebook Ads allow targeting specific demographics or keywords relevant to your niche—maximizing chances for conversions.

A word of caution, though: Paid advertising requires careful planning and constant monitoring to avoid overspending without seeing sufficient returns. Make sure you understand how these platforms work before jumping in headfirst.

An example worth mentioning is Neil Patel, one of today's most successful digital marketers, who managed his way up using both organic SEO strategies and paid advertising campaigns effectively.

"Your goal should never be getting 'more' traffic, but rather 'better' quality ones," Neil Patel once said.

Analyzing this quote reveals why many affiliates fail to generate meaningful revenue despite attracting large amounts of visits: They focus too much on numbers rather than visitors' relevancy or intent.

Case studies have shown time after time that using multiple channels concurrently increases overall success rates with affiliate marketing efforts due to its compound effect over time (referencing 'Integrated Marketing Communication,' Journal of Marketing Theory and Practice).

Diversify Your Strategy

Diversify your strategy by leveraging multiple channels concurrently for the best results—don't put all eggs in one basket!

When looking at ways to drive more eyeballs:

- Consider guest blogging opportunities
- Leverage email marketing
- Engage with followers across all major social media platforms
- Regularly updated blog posts with fresh information
- Incorporate videos into the content strategy

Content Has Value

Every piece of content has potential value toward achieving better search rankings and increasing visibility online—make each count!

Search Engine Land reports show an over 60% increase in organic click-through rates achieved through effective SEO practices alone (2018 data). Moreover, according to the Business Insider Intelligence 2020 report, email drives $38 ROI per $1 spent, while Social Media Today states that 80% of B2C businesses find social media an effective channel for driving customer acquisition—providing every approach holds merit if employed properly!

Numbers Don't Lie

Numbers don't lie! Implementing proper SEO techniques, smart use of email marketing, and active participation in social media will result in undeniable growth in website visits, boosting potential commission earnings significantly!

To achieve the desired outcome, follow these steps:

1. Identify target audience characteristics and preferences
2. Optimize website structure and speed
3. Create engaging content regularly based on relevant topics or keywords
4. Actively engage with the audience across various platforms
5. Monitor performance metrics closely, making necessary adjustments over time

Remember: Consistency is key! Stay committed to long-term results, which will surely follow suit eventually!

Search Engine Optimization (SEO)

Demystifying SEO: The Key to Becoming Visible

The internet is a vast ocean, and your affiliate marketing website is but a tiny boat amidst its waves. But fear not, because just as the lighthouse guides ships in darkness, Search Engine Optimization (SEO) illuminates the path for your site to become discoverable.

For those who are new to this term, SEO is a process that helps improve your website's visibility on search engines like Google. It's an essential tool in the digital world that can help you stand out from millions of other sites vying for attention. And no, it's not magic; it's science mixed with some art.

Now, let's dive deeper into SEO and unravel its mysteries.

Search engine algorithms have evolved over time and now consider hundreds of factors before ranking websites. Some aspects they consider include relevance, quality of content, page load speed, mobile friendliness, and user interaction with the site. This may seem daunting at first glance, but don't worry; we'll go through these elements one by one.

SEO Strategies and Techniques

SEO involves various strategies and techniques aimed at improving a website's visibility on search engines for relevant searches. Some of these include the following:

Keyword optimization: This is the practice of strategically using words or phrases users type when searching online. You can achieve this by following the steps below:

- Ensure you are optimizing the right keywords. Ensure that your efforts are worth it and that you can rank easily. This step is possibly the most difficult, which is why I want to cover it first. You need to estimate the amount of traffic other pages are getting; this will give you an idea of the amount of traffic you could potentially get when you use the right keywords.

- When using certain keywords on your website, ensure they can bring in valuable traffic. Decide what the purpose of the keywords is. Are you trying to make sales, make others aware of your brand, or do you want to increase your number of subscribers?

- You might come across keywords that are difficult to rank for. You need to take an in-depth look at the number of unique domains in order to get an overview of this. The number of linking domains increases the difficulty of ranking.

- You should also look at why people are using those keywords to search the internet. The main reason why people head over to the internet is usually to learn new things, purchase a new product, or find a website they saw somewhere. This is important if you want to optimize the keywords you are using. Doing this will help you establish whether you are able to provide your audience with the things they are looking for.

Think of search intent: There are three Cs with regard to search intent, including the following:

- Content type: These are the types of websites audiences are looking for, including blog posts, product pages, category pages, and landing pages. You need to look at which content type is most sought-after and then create content around that.

- Content format: This is information about how readers want their content to be shown to them. These include DIY guides, step-by-step guides, list posts, your opinion, product reviews and comparisons, and product ranges.

- Content angle: This revolves around the selling point of each piece of content. The content should be interesting for your audience, and it should match the topic.

Follow on-page SEO: Once the above steps have been completed, you can start writing your content with SEO in mind. This will help your readers understand and absorb the information you are giving them. There are also various online tools you can use to help you find the right tags, images, etc., to optimize your content and make it more relatable to your audience.

Another technique involves creating backlinks. These are links from other websites leading to yours, which signal to search engines that your site offers valuable information.

However, keywords and backlinks are just one part of the equation. Creating high-quality content that real people find useful remains pivotal in achieving good rankings on search engines—enter "content is king." But remember not to stuff keywords mindlessly into your content, as it could lead to penalties from Google!

Content isn't King; it's the Kingdom. –Lee Odden

On-Page and Off-Page Strategies

Analyzing our topic further reveals two main categories of SEO: On-page and off-page. On-page refers to actions taken within your website, such as optimizing title tags or images, while off-page mainly deals with external factors like earning backlinks or social signals pointing toward your site.

A case study published by Moz highlighted how Buffer experienced a 4x increase in traffic within two months after implementing an effective off-page strategy involving guest blogging across reputable platforms.

These strategies are crucial to improving a website's ranking on search engines.

Here are some interesting points about SEO you might want to jot down:

- Quality beats quantity when it comes to backlinks.
- Mobile-friendly design can boost rankings.
- Long-form content tends to perform better than short ones.

Implementing Technical Changes

This includes improving page load speed and producing engaging content, which significantly improves rankings. You can review previous chapters to get more in-depth details on this topic.

Accordingly, BridgeEdge research found that organic searches were responsible for over 53% of all trackable web traffic, indicating how important good rankings are for visibility online.

Higher Visibility Leads

This directly translates into higher traffic, eventually converting into more sales opportunities! To start seeing results from SEO efforts: (You can review previous chapters for more detail on these points.)

1. Start by conducting keyword research using tools like Google Keyword Planner or SEMRush.

2. Create unique and engaging long-form content around these keywords.

3. Ensure meta-tags (title and description) incorporate target keywords naturally.

4. Improve page-load speeds via compression or caching methods.

5. Earn high-quality backlinks through guest posting or influencer collaboration.

Remember, patience is key here! Results often take time since many factors influence rankings simultaneously, so test different strategies until you hit gold!

In conclusion, despite seeming complex initially, once understood correctly, SEO can be harnessed effectively even by beginners, enabling them to outshine their competition online!

Converting Visitors Into Buyers

The key to converting visitors into buyers is not only about the product or service but also about understanding and addressing customers' needs, desires, concerns, and objections. —Ian Lurie

As an affiliate marketer, your primary goal is to convert your website's visitors into buyers. This isn't simply about convincing people to click on a link; it's about guiding them through a process known as the sales funnel.

In essence, the sales funnel represents the journey potential customers take from when they first interact with you until they make a purchase. It's called a 'funnel' because it starts broad (with many prospects) and narrows down (too few conversions). Understanding and mastering this concept is crucial to ethical affiliate marketing.

Sales funnels aren't new. In fact, they've been around since the early days of direct mail marketing. What's changed over time is how these funnels are built and optimized, thanks to advances in digital technology.

Now, let's dive deeper into optimizing your sales funnel for maximum conversion rates.

Understanding Customer Psychology

To maximize conversions, understanding customer psychology is paramount. Knowing what motivates your audience can help you craft compelling offers that will be hard for them to resist.

The foundation of any successful sales funnel lies in understanding consumer behavior. People don't just buy products or services; they buy solutions to their problems, status symbols, experiences, feelings, and the emotional benefits that come along with them. Customers want to have a personalized experience, so making them feel like you are only tending to them can give positive results.

Evidence shows us that emotions heavily influence purchasing decisions, more than logical factors like price or features. So, when creating content or crafting offers for your affiliate marketing efforts, tap into these emotional triggers.

For example, if you're promoting fitness equipment as an affiliate marketer, rather than simply listing product specifications like size and weight capacity, talk about how owning such equipment could lead to a healthier lifestyle or increased self-confidence due to improved physical appearance.

Remember this quote from Zig Ziglar: "People don't buy for logical reasons. They buy for emotional reasons." This highlights why understanding consumer psychology is vital to converting visitors into buyers.

Another way to improve your conversion rates is to create content that will educate your audience and give them the information they are looking for. You need to be able to answer all the questions your audience might have when they visit your platform. When creating informative content, ensure the information is easy to understand so you don't lose your audience's interest.

To further improve conversion rates in your sales funnel, consider employing techniques like creating compelling Calls-to-Action (CTAs) and optimizing landing pages.

A study published by Marketing Experiments (n.d.) found that CTAs with action-oriented text performed better than those without it, which means that using verbs like "get," "try," and "discover" can increase conversion rates compared to passive phrases like "learn more."

Moreover, according to HubSpot (2023), research data from four million landing pages across different industries showed that personalized CTAs converted 202% better than default versions! By customizing CTAs based on visitor data like location or browsing history, you can make them feel more relevant, thus increasing their chances of engagement, which ultimately leads to conversion.

Ensure that you offer various prices on your platforms so your audience can compare which is best for them. They will also be able to see what they get, depending on the price they want to pay. Using this strategy will also help you bundle up some of your products to increase your profits.

The last strategy you can use within the psychology of your buyers is to make them feel part of your company and a community. Craft your offers in a way that will make them feel like part of your group, like creating content that tells your customers they will be one of 100 lucky customers to get a free product when they purchase it for the first time.

Crafting Compelling CTAs

Crafting compelling call-to-actions, or CTAs, and personalizing landing pages based on user data can significantly boost conversion rates. CTAs are made to encourage customers to take specific action on their journey in your business. This could be anything from joining your newsletter mailing list, completing a contact form, or making a purchase.

You will improve your social media engagement, have more leads, and increase conversions when you build a well-thought-out CTA. This means that it is more than just putting a button on your platform and expecting your potential customers to click on it. There is no one-size-fits-all CTA; it all depends on your business and your marketing strategy. There are a few different types of CTAs you can use, including the following:

- Button CTAs: These are buttons strategically placed on your platform that include actions like 'Shop Now', or 'Download Now."

- Text CTAs: These are links placed on your site that take your audience to a certain page to have them take action.

- Image CTAs: These are specifically designed with links built in to have an audience take action.

- Pop-up CTAs: When you visit a site, and you see a box come up when you are ready to exit the site, that is a pop-up CTA. It reminds your audience to take action before they leave or before they do something else.

- Form CTAs: These CTAs encourage your audience to submit their information on the form that comes up on your site.

- Social Media CTAs: These are social media links you add to your site to encourage your audience to follow you on your social media sites.

- Below are some valuable tips to help you create a CTA that will help you reach business success.

- Know your audience: In order to craft the right CTAs, you need to understand your audience and what they want from your site. You need to take their needs, pain points, and motivations into consideration.

- Create urgency and FOMO: Creating a sense of urgency with your CTAs will encourage readers to take action now rather than later. It increases the fear of missing out (FOMO) reaction people have when they see an offer that looks intriguing.

- Make it look attractive: The CTAs you create need to make your audience want to click on your link to take action. Do some research on colors, fonts, and buttons to help you find the right combinations.

- Use social proof: Gather some testimonials or reviews from other customers to show your audience the value others have received from signing up for your unique offer.

- Make it relevant: Your call to action needs to be relevant to the content of your site. For example, you might add a CTA that takes your audience to your ebook about email marketing downloading page if your site is related to email marketing.

- Strategically place it: Your CTA needs to be in a place where your audience will be able to see it when visiting your site.

- Test and optimize: Test out the different types of CTAs mentioned above to see if they are working or not. If you find that one isn't working, then switch it up and try another one. This is the best way to ensure you are getting the action you want from your audience.

Interesting Bullet Points:

- Action-oriented CTAs perform better than passive ones.

- Personalized CTAs convert almost twice as much compared to default versions.

A/B Testing

A/B testing or split testing should be used frequently throughout all stages of your sales funnel optimization process, from headline creation down to CTA design. Nothing should be left untested! A/B tests let you see which elements of your website are improving the impact it has on your audience and which ones should be changed to increase it.

According to statistics compiled by Invesp (n.d.), companies whose conversion rates improved last year were performing an average of two A/B test variations per month!

A detailed step-by-step action plan might look something like this:

1. Define Your Buyer's Persona: Understand who exactly you are targeting. What are their pain points? What motivates them?

2. Craft Compelling Offers and Content: Use the psychological principles we discussed earlier here while creating content or offers that resonate well with customers' emotions rather than just logic alone.

3. Create compelling and action-oriented CTAs: Use strong, persuasive language that incites action immediately.

4. Personalize landing pages based on user data: Make wise use of available user data, making every interaction count.

Ensure that you follow these steps with extreme detail to get the most out of your A/B testing so you can improve your platform where needed.

Repeat

Diligently follow each step mentioned above, religiously iterating processes wherever necessary based on results observed via frequent testing, thereby ensuring continuous improvement, always leading towards higher conversions eventually.

Chapter 7:

Advanced Affiliate Marketing Strategies and Using Email Marketing

The secret of change is to focus all your energy not on fighting the old but on building the new. —Socrates.

An affiliate marketer's journey is akin to a tree's life cycle. The seed (your core idea) is planted in the fertile soil of the market. It sprouts into a sapling (relevant content and trustworthiness), gaining strength over time with the right nourishment. But as it grows taller towards the sky, it faces stronger winds and storms (ever-changing market trends, competition, and ethical dilemmas).

Just like how trees change their growth strategies based on their environment but stay true to their nature, do you, as an affiliate marketer, need to change your business to adjust to changing circumstances? Keep in mind that even as you change your strategies, your integrity should remain unchanged and unshaken if you want to hold on to your ethical business.

Albert Einstein once said, "Whoever is careless with the truth in small matters cannot be trusted with important things." This applies perfectly to affiliate marketers. Your readers trust you for authentic reviews and advice; misleading them for short-term gains can permanently tarnish your reputation.

Let's delve into maintaining an ethical approach amidst changing circumstances:

1. Transparency is key: Always disclose your affiliations clearly before promoting products or services. Honesty will solidify trust among audiences.

2. Prioritize Quality Over Quantity: Promote only products you have used before or have a strong belief in.

3. Respect Privacy: Do not misuse personal data collected from subscribers for unethical practices.

4. Continuous Learning: Stay updated about the latest FTC affiliate marketing guidelines.

If trouble brews stronger than anticipated, for example, if a product you promoted turns out to be defective, then you need to sincerely apologize and take the necessary corrective measures immediately to rectify the situation.

Key Idea: Growing as an affiliate marketer involves mastering new strategies while maintaining consistent honesty and transparency.

Success Stories

Now, let's turn to some inspiring stories from successful yet ethical marketers:

Jane has been running a fitness blog for five years now. She promotes only organic supplements through her platform after trying them personally. Despite numerous lucrative efforts from synthetic supplement manufacturers, Jane has always prioritized her readers' health over monetary gains.

Another example is Mike, who runs a tech review channel on YouTube. He recently found out that one of his affiliates was selling refurbished items as new ones without informing customers about it.

Instead of ignoring this issue to avoid losing commission money, he cut ties with them immediately, announcing his decision publicly.

Darren is possibly one of the most successful affiliate marketers to date. He is always sharing his success, techniques, and the history of his business with potential future affiliate marketers. Darren started his business at a very young age and has managed to make nearly half a million dollars in revenue in 10 years. He never leaves a stone unturned when recommending products to his audience, and he makes sure to check that his customers are satisfied with the products they purchase.

These stories confirm that staying honest might seem challenging initially but eventually leads to sustainable success by creating a loyal customer base.

Advanced Strategies

There are a few strategies you can use to ensure your affiliate business is successful. These include the following:

Create content before you launch: Ensuring you have existing content when you launch your website will give you an advantage in the world of affiliate marketing. Create at least 20 articles before you launch your platform and have existing affiliate partners by your side. Stay MacNaught (2023) says the following: "Over the last two years, by far the greatest performing site for us has been those where we'd created 20-plus pieces of content before putting a website live."

- Have different affiliate partners: Diversifying your affiliate partners will protect you against the possibility of the companies refusing to pay, closing down, or cutting down on commission payouts. You will lose a significant amount of profits when this happens, and with diversification, you can prevent this.

- Build a relationship with your audience: This is especially important when your various accounts or your platform are hacked, deleted, or reported. This means you will lose contact with your audience. You need to build relationships with your audience from your platform to ensure you have contact with them should the inevitable happen.

- Recommend your audience's products: Consider recommending the products your audience is looking for. If your audience is asking you for a specific product, then you might want to take some time to do your research and find an affiliate program for it. This will help you build your relationship with your client while making a profit. It will also help you build your credibility and trust.

- Know your product: One of the most important aspects of affiliate marketing is knowing the products you are recommending in and out. You will always get customers who have a million questions, and you need to be able to answer these questions if you want to make a sale.

- Disclose your affiliate links: Telling your audience you are affiliated with a specific product or company, and you are earning a commission will help you build trust with your audience. You risk alienating your customers or losing their trust if you don't disclose the fact that you are receiving commission, and your audience learns this somewhere else. Keep in mind that the Federal Trade Commission (FTC) also has strict rules with regard to recommending products.

- Share discount codes: You have the freedom to ask your affiliate partners whether they have discount codes for you to share with your audience. These codes can be shared on your social media, via email marketing, or on your platform, or you can add a discount meta description when creating your CTA.

- Utilize Instagram: A platform is a great way to get your affiliate marketing business started, but it might not be completely necessary. You can start an Instagram account and recommend products on your page for viewers to make a purchase.

- Product reviews and tutorials: Product reviews are highly sought after by various people who are interested in making a purchase of a product. Writing these reviews can increase the likelihood of you making sales and receiving profits. The key to writing reviews is using keywords about the product you are writing about to optimize the chances of your audience seeing the review.

- Research trending topics: Most people follow the trends set by others. Keeping track of changing trends can help you take your affiliate business to the next level. Do regular research on popular keywords to give you an indication of what your audience might be looking for if you want to remain competitive.

- Run ads: Creating and running specific ads can help you with your affiliate marketing. This means taking time to create ads for seasons like Christmas, Valentine's Day, and even Easter. These are just some of the holidays most people want to buy products for, so creating ads for these seasons will increase your conversion rates and make you noticeable.

Now that you have some valuable strategies you can use in your affiliate marketing business, let's move on to email marketing and how to use it to improve your reach.

Email Marketing

Email has an ability many channels don't: creating valuable, personal touches - at scale. –David Newman

But I don't want to spam my customers, you protest; *I hate receiving emails myself!* Here's the twist: email marketing isn't about spamming. It's about relationship-building.

Let's imagine your online business as a bustling city market. Your website is your colorful stall, filled with enticing products that make passersby stop and look. But these people won't all buy on their first visit; they're just browsing, comparing, and perhaps waiting for payday. An email list is like a friendly shopkeeper who remembers faces and preferences; it keeps the conversation going until they're ready to commit.

Science proves this analogy true. According to McKinsey and Company (n.d.), people who purchase products marketed through email spend 138% more than those who do not receive such offers. That's a powerful reason why building an ethical email list should be at the heart of your affiliate marketing strategy.

So, how do we go about it?

The Ethics of Collecting Emails

Paint yourself as a trustworthy shopkeeper and not a pushy salesman. Ensure each person willingly provides their email address by using opt-in forms on your website or blog post footers with clear guidance on what subscribers can expect from you (weekly newsletters? Exclusive discounts?). Never ever buy lists or trick users into subscribing—honesty always wins in the long run.

Segmentation for Personalization

Imagine sending your vegetarian friend an invitation to a barbecue cookout—awkward! One-size-fits-all marketing gives similar vibes and is impersonal and off-putting. This is where segmentation comes in handy.

By dividing up your audience based on interests, past purchases, or demographics (like age and location), you can tailor content that speaks directly to them, resulting in better engagement rates.

Breakout Box

Key Idea: An ethically obtained subscriber list allows for personalized communication between you and potential customers, leading to stronger relationships.

Email has an ability many channels don't: creating valuable personal touches - at scale. –David Newman

Now let's dive into some actionable steps:

1. Create Valuable Content: Offer something irresistible, like an eBook or exclusive discount codes, in exchange for signing up.

2. Optimize Opt-In Forms: Make them easy to spot yet non-intrusive.

3. Use Double Opt-In: Send new subscribers an email asking them to confirm their subscription, ensuring only interested parties join.

4. Segment Your List: Use data analytics tools available with most email services.

5. Personalize Emails: Include recipients' names and use segment-specific language.

If things still seem daunting, consider hiring professional help; there are companies specializing in ethical list building.

Lastly, here's some food for thought:

Common enemy? "Spray-and-pray email."

Ah-ha moment? Segmentation equals personalization equals trust equals sales!

Key Takeaways

- Ethical list building fosters meaningful customer relationships.

- Segmentation allows personalized communication, increasing the chances of conversion.

- Always ask permission before adding someone to your mailing list.

- Provide value in every interaction.

Remember, in ethical affiliate marketing, success stems from respect for the individuals behind each click—or rather, each email!

Chapter 8:

Monitoring Performance and Scaling Your Business

What gets measured gets improved. –Peter Drucker

Affiliate marketing is much like a living organism. It evolves, grows, adapts to its environment, and needs regular check-ups to ensure its health is at its best. If you're at the helm of an affiliate marketing campaign, your role is akin to that of a doctor. You must monitor performance diligently, make necessary adjustments promptly, and keep your finger on the pulse of market trends.

In all my years studying and practicing affiliate marketing, I've found it's not enough just to set up a campaign and let it run its course. You need data-driven insights into how well your efforts are performing. This can be done through metrics such as click-through rates or conversion rates. The crucial information allows you to identify what works best for your audience and adjust accordingly.

Monitoring Performance

Let's delve deeper into the heart of performance monitoring. Tracking tools are indispensable here; these software solutions provide real-time data about how users interact with your affiliate links, products, or services you promote. Google Analytics is one such tool that offers comprehensive insights about user behavior on your website.

Key Takeaway: Tools like Google Analytics offer invaluable insights into user behavior on your website, which aids in strategic decision-making.

On top of these digital diagnostic tests, there's another side to tracking performance that analyzes the collected data effectively for decision-making purposes. This involves identifying patterns in user behavior over time, recognizing what drives conversions most efficiently, or understanding why certain strategies failed.

For instance, if you notice a sharp decline in traffic from one source but an increase from another after implementing a new strategy, that's valuable insight! It signals where you may need adjustments or improvements to optimize results.

Now let's bring some real-world perspective into our discussion with examples from successful affiliate marketers who have excelled at performance monitoring:

1. **Pat Flynn**: A renowned online entrepreneur who built his entire empire largely through ethical affiliate marketing practices. He uses detailed monthly income reports as part of his strategy review process, which he shares publicly on his blog, "Smart Passive Income." These reports help him understand which strategies work best so he can adjust his future accordingly.

2. **Matthew Woodward**: An award-winning blogger known for his transparent case studies documenting every step taken towards achieving success in different areas, including affiliate marketing.

Albert Einstein once said, "The measure of intelligence is the ability to change." This quote holds true, especially when we talk about adjusting our strategies based on insightful analysis and market trends.

Analyzing past performances isn't sufficient, though; being aware of current market trends also plays a pivotal role while making adjustments because what worked yesterday might not necessarily work today due to constantly changing consumer behaviors.

Regular Strategy Updates

Regularly updating strategies based on market trends ensures continued success.

Next up are some interesting or quick tips gathered throughout my experience:

Use Multiple Analytics Tools for More Comprehensive Data

Before choosing a data analytics tool for your business, you need to be aware of the various key factors you need to consider. You need to take the type of data you want to analyze into consideration and whether you will be sharing the information with other companies.

The various analytics tools you might come across can gather either quantitative or qualitative data from stores and business processes. These programs then study the information to help you make the right decision for your business. You can combine the tools you use, for example, a statistical tool, a predictive modeling tool, and a data mining tool, to help you get the most comprehensive data. These tools will not only help you increase your performance, but also your profitability and productivity.

I would recommend that you use business analytics software as opposed to Business Intelligence (BI) software, as business analytics digs deeper into the data it collects and can show you any flaws, alert policies, how to resolve potential issues, and help you predict any future changes, including results.

Some of the most popular data analytics software include (Sramek, 2021):

- Scaleo: an Affiliate marketing software

- Google Analytics

- Forensiq: a platform that detects fraud

- Mailchimp: software that helps you with email marketing and analytics

- Hootsuite: helps you with social marketing analysis

- Microsoft Power BI: a business intelligence tool

- SAS: another business intelligence tool

- Tableau: BI tool

- SEMrush: a tool to assist you with your SEO

- Excel: The most used spreadsheet on the market

These tools are all extremely helpful in your affiliate marketing business, but you should do your research on each of them before using one.

Conduct A/B Testing Regularly

This topic was discussed in the previous chapter, and I would like to refresh your memory about just how important it is to do regular A/B testing. A/B testing can help you look at similar marketing campaigns and conversion rates so you can change your strategy to improve your business. You can achieve this by running different versions of the same strategy and seeing which one works best.

Keep Track of Industry News and Updates

Staying updated about news and trends in the affiliate marketing world can help you increase your conversion rates because you will be tending to your audience's needs. This topic has been discussed before and should be remembered if you want to be successful in your business endeavors.

Making Adjustments

Once you have completed your performance analysis, it's important to start testing some other strategies. Doing this will help you see which strategies will work best for your business so you can reach success.

Achieving Optimal Results

To achieve optimal results, continuously learn and adapt based on analytical insights. This means that you need to be willing to change as the markets change and adjust your strategies as needed.

According to Statista.com (n.d.), as of Q4 2020, approx. 81% of advertisers leveraged Affiliate Marketing Programs for procurement or engagement purposes, whereas around 84% of publishers utilized this channel, showing its growing popularity amongst parties involved.

Being Proactive

Being proactive with performance monitoring will give you an edge in this highly competitive space.

Take note of the following action steps:

1. Pick suitable tracking tools according to business needs.
2. Set Key Performance Indicators (KPIs)
3. Regularly analyze the gathered data
4. Identify successful patterns and strategies and replicate them
5. Stay updated with the latest industry trends
6. Implement changes swiftly whenever needed

Remember, success lies not just in setting sail but also in navigating effectively by adapting swiftly based on winds (market trends), waves (consumer demands), and weather conditions (competition). So embrace change and stay ahead!

Scaling Your Business

> *Revenue is king. Tying your content to revenue and lead generation is critical to success.* –Elizabeth Clor

The key to affiliate marketing is always scaling your business so you can reach new heights and get in contact with new audiences. The amount of money you make with your business is in your hands and depends on the steps you take. So right now, you might be wondering how you can scale your business so you can build it to amazing heights. I want to discuss the top 12 ways in which you can scale your business and increase your profits:

- **Increase Your Content:** The one sure way to scale your business is by creating more content. This will increase your visibility even more and the likelihood of your links being clicked on. The more content you create for your affiliate business, the higher the possibility of it popping up in search engine results.

- **Aggressively Promote Your Content:** The more content you create, the more aggressively you need to advertise it so it can be seen by your audience. There are various ways you can accomplish this, but the most effective way is through blogging, social media outreach programs, and paid advertising. You should focus your time and energy on getting your content in front of the eyes of as many viewers as possible to increase your reach.

- **Increased Conversion Rates:** Optimizing your conversion rate means you will turn as many visitors into purchasing clients as possible. The most effective way of accomplishing this is to create a call-to-action button on both your social media pages and website. You may also consider adding bonuses to incentivize your customers to make a purchase.

- **Utilize New Traffic Sources:** As mentioned earlier, social media is a powerful way of introducing your affiliate business to new people. You can share your affiliate links on various social media platforms like Facebook, Twitter, Quora, TikTok, Instagram, Pinterest, Medium, and YouTube. Post regularly while avoiding the chance of being reported for spamming other people.

- **Become a Master at Paid Traffic:** Using paid traffic is another great way to make your business visible to potential customers. Paid advertisements require an initial investment, but it is guaranteed that you will maximize your returns. You should, however, still ensure you are using the right keywords, or you might not show up in search results. As your business grows, ensure that you adjust your advertising budget so you can optimize paid traffic. One thing to keep in mind with paid traffic is that you need to stay educated and up-to-date with trends, or you might be burning through your budget faster than expected.

- **Collaborate:** You don't always have to compete with other affiliate marketers. Instead, get in contact with other affiliates and build your relationships with them. You will never know what you are able to learn from them to scale your business. You can also collaborate with them and guest stars on their blog posts or podcasts to increase your visibility among their audience. Always remember to keep the value you are providing your audience in mind.

- **Diversify:** Diversifying the products you are offering your customers is the best way to optimize the profits you are getting. You can take a look at various products in your niche and introduce as many as possible to your audience. In other words, take your eggs and place them in various baskets instead of gathering everything in one basket.

- **Target Profitable Keywords:** Do some research on keywords your audience might use when searching for content on the internet. This includes using keywords that have buyer intent and creating content that is both commercial and informative.

- **Review Your Products:** Take a look at the sales each of your products is making and adjust so you can compile the right combination to suit your audience. This will help you increase sales, especially if your audience feels your content is directly related to them. If you are selling digital products, then you want to add more high-ticket items to the platforms you use. If you prefer selling physical items through your affiliate links, then you need to look at products within your niche that have a higher profit.

- **Take a Step Back:** When running promotions, are you constantly using the same promotion, or are you looking for ways to improve on your existing promotions? Take some time to review this and make the necessary adjustments. Ensure that you are adding different discounts and promotions on your platform or offering free shipping to convince individuals to make a purchase.

- **Prioritize Quality:** Within the affiliate marketing industry, quantity is never more important than quality, especially when you are attempting to scale your business. Instead of filling your content with various low-quality products, focus on a handful of high-quality products to offer your audience. This will not only help you increase your profits, but you will also be able to build trust, credibility, and reliability with your audience.

- **Build a Team:** When attempting to scale your business, don't be afraid to hire some more help. You could look for a virtual assistant to help you with your administrative duties or hire someone to help you with your content creation. There is no shame in admitting that the work gets too much at times. Hiring someone to help you will also free up some valuable time you can use to build your business and focus more on customer service.

As you can see, scaling your business has various topics, not just one. At the end of the day, educating yourself should be your first priority so you can stay ahead of the market and your competition.

Chapter 9:

Legal Considerations And Ethics

Honesty is paramount to building customer trust and loyalty. –Anik Singal "The Circle of Profit"

When you venture into the affiliate marketing world, you may find yourself standing at a crossroads. On one side lies the path of quick profits and dubious practices, while on the other stands the road to ethical business conduct. It's easy to be swayed by the short-term benefits of questionable tactics but remember that your choices will shape your immediate future and determine your long-term success.

The concept of ethics is often overlooked in online businesses. However, it plays an integral role in determining any company's reputation and credibility. Ethics refers to moral principles that govern a person or group's behavior, which means they define what is right and wrong. Ethics can range from respecting customer privacy to providing accurate advertising information in an online business context.

Unethical practices might provide temporary success but can have disastrous consequences for your brand image in the long run. False advertising, for instance, might attract some initial customers, but once they realize they've been misled, their trust will be irreparable. Not only will they stop patronizing your products or services, but word-of-mouth about these experiences can deter potential clients, leading to significant losses over time.

Conversely, practicing transparency and honesty yields several benefits for your business's growth. When customers know what they're getting into, whether it relates to product specifications or terms of service, they appreciate honesty, fostering loyalty towards your brand.

Honesty Isn't Just Morally Correct

Honesty isn't just good for your morals; it's good for business too! Several studies back up this claim! Research conducted by Label Insight found that 94% of consumers are likely to show loyalty to a brand that offers complete transparency (Nguyen, 2022).

Let's consider Amazon as an example: how did this e-commerce giant become so successful? Sure, their vast product selection played a part in it, but what truly set them apart was their commitment to open communication with customers via authentic reviews and customer-friendly return policies—a clear demonstration of ethical practice.

> *In looking for people to hire, look for three qualities: integrity, intelligence, and energy.* –Warren Buffett.

Buffett's words perfectly encapsulate why businesses should prioritize ethical values; without integrity (or ethics), intelligence and energy are useless when building customer trust.

So, how do we apply these principles practically? Let's look at Pat Flynn from Smart Passive Income, a well-known affiliate marketer renowned for his transparency disclosure statements accompanying all his affiliate links, a practice he believes has significantly bolstered his audience's trust!

Transparency builds trust and is the cornerstone of any successful relationship, business or otherwise! Here are some bullet points summarizing the key ideas related to building trust:

- Ethics refers to moral principles governing behavior.
- Unethical practices damage brand reputations immensely.
- Transparency fosters customer loyalty.
- Authenticity contributes positively toward overall business growth.

Ethical Values Isn't a Preference

Practicing ethical values isn't merely a preference; it's imperative for securing long-term success!

Accordingly, a report by The Forum Corporation indicates that companies maintaining high standards of ethical behavior outperform those who don't by nearly 300% (Mahlaka, 2022).

incorporate these insights into action steps:

1. **Incorporate Transparency:** Clearly state all terms and conditions related to products or services offered, including any associated costs or fees, to ensure informed decision-making on the part of customers.

2. **Prioritize Customer Privacy:** Respect data privacy norms strictly, and never misuse personal customer data acquired during transactions or processes.

3. **Maintain Authentic Communication Channels:** Provide platforms where consumers can voice their opinions and concerns freely with prompt redressal mechanisms implemented promptly.

4. **Promote Fair Advertising Practices:** Avoid deceptive or false advertising. Clearly describe what exactly is being sold or offered without exaggerations or misrepresentations involved.

In conclusion, ethical practices aren't optional; they're essential elements contributing towards sustainable growth strategies and ensuring longevity within competitive business landscapes!

Defining Ethics in Online Businesses

Affiliate marketing has made businesses millions and ordinary people millionaires.
—Bo Bennett

In a world where digital technology reigns, it's no surprise that affiliate marketing has become an integral part of today's business landscape. But what exactly is affiliate marketing? And more importantly, why should we be concerned about ethics in this field?

Think of affiliate marketing as a modern interpretation of the age-old practice of commission-based sales. It involves promoting products or services offered by other companies and earning a percentage from any sales that occur via your referral. It's like being an enthusiastic friend who recommends a great restaurant to another friend, only to receive a complimentary meal as thanks.

The Impact of Unethical Practices on Brand Reputation and Growth

So, where does the element of ethics come into play? Well, in our restaurant scenario, imagine if you were recommending this place not because you genuinely loved their food but because they promised you free meals for every customer you sent their way. Suddenly, there seems to be a conflict between personal gain and honest recommendation.

The same applies to affiliate marketing; ethical practices are critical for maintaining transparency and trust with your audience. Unfortunately, unethical behavior can creep in when marketers promote low-quality products just for high commissions or mislead consumers about their relationship with the products or company.

Key Idea: Ethical affiliate marketing focuses on honesty and transparency while providing value to consumers through meaningful product recommendations.

Understanding These Aspects

Why is understanding this fundamental aspect so crucial? Because it forms the bedrock upon which successful and ethical affiliate marketing strategies are built!

Let's take an example from science: Newton's First Law states that an object at rest stays at rest unless acted upon by an external force. Could we consider unethical practices as that disruptive force diverting us off course?

To stay on track toward success in affiliate marketing:

- Always disclose your relationships.

- Be sincere in your recommendations.

- Don't compromise quality for high commissions.

If things get extra bad and you've been involved in questionable practices, don't lose heart! Take immediate steps towards damage control: make public apologies if needed, retract misleading information, and most importantly, learn from your mistakes!

Remember the following quote:

Ethics is knowledge, the difference between what you have a right to do and what is right to do. —Potter Stewart.

So, let's outline those key points:

1. Affiliate marketing is essentially commission-based sales done digitally.

2. Ethics play a vital role in maintaining consumer trust.

3. Adhere strictly to guidelines, disclose relationships clearly, recommend sincerely, and prioritize quality over profit.

4. If caught up in unethical activities, apologize publicly if necessary and rectify mistakes as soon as possible.

Benefits of Practicing Transparency and Honesty

By grasping these fundamentals, we set ourselves up for success within ethical boundaries, thus creating sustainable businesses that stand on solid ground rather than shaky foundations! So, hop aboard as we delve deeper into this fascinating world filled with opportunities yet fraught with challenges requiring careful navigation!

> *Your reputation is more important than your paycheck, and your integrity is worth more than your career.* –Ryan Freitas

Welcome to the world of affiliate marketing, a realm where creativity meets commerce. However, as you delve deeper into this digital domain, it's essential to remember that there's more than just catchy and strategic SEO at play. A significant aspect that often gets overlooked is the legal framework governing online businesses.

The labyrinthine landscape of legal regulations may seem daunting initially, but fear not; with a bit of guidance and understanding, you can navigate through these legalities with relative ease. First, you must grasp the importance of Terms of Service (TOS) agreements. These are contracts between your business and its users or customers, outlining their rights and responsibilities. They provide an essential layer of protection for your business against potential disputes or liabilities.

Let's delve further into the main body of our guide, starting with privacy policies and the General Data Protection Regulations (GDPR). GDPR is a set of laws introduced by the European Union in 2018 aimed at protecting EU citizens' online data. Even if your business isn't based in Europe, if you have EU visitors or customers, GDPR also applies to you. The essence lies in transparency about how customer data is collected, used, protected, or shared.

Terms of Service (TOS) Agreements

TOS agreements offer protection against potential disputes while maintaining transparency about user rights and responsibilities aids in compliance with GDRP regulations.

One might wonder why terms like "privacy policy" keep popping up so frequently. This document informs users what personal information your website collects from them and how it uses it. In creating an effective privacy policy, make sure it covers all bases—what information is being gathered, who has access to this data, how long it will be stored for, etcetera.

Moving on to another vital area: FTC guidelines for disclosure and endorsements. As an affiliate marketer, promoting third-party products or services on your platform for a commission fee means adhering strictly to the Federal Trade Commission's (FTC) guidelines for endorsements. The FTC mandates clear disclosure when endorsing products or services received either free of charge or through sponsorship deals.

The only place success comes before work is in the dictionary. –Vince Lombardi

This quote perfectly encapsulates our topic because navigating these legal aspects requires effort but ultimately paves the way toward sustainable success.

Now let's assess some solutions to understand these concepts better:

One solution could be hiring a lawyer specializing in Internet law who can guide you through creating comprehensive TOS agreements and privacy policies besides ensuring compliance with FTC rules and GDPR regulations.

Case Studies

Take the Amazon Affiliates Program as an example; they require affiliates to clearly disclose their association using specific language defined by them; non-compliance leads affiliates to lose out on earned commissions! Another example could be Google's pending fines imposed on websites violating GDPR rules, resulting in substantial fines, proving that ignorance isn't bliss when dealing with cyber laws!

Professional Assistance

Having professional assistance can simplify navigation around complex legislation and prevent potential pitfalls leading to hefty penalties.

Here are some points summarizing key aspects:

Understanding TOS Agreements: An affiliate program's terms of service agreement is a legal document stating the relationship between the company offering the affiliate program and the affiliate (you). A comprehensive agreement will have different sections outlining various points to ensure both parties are on the same page.

Some of the sections that should be included in this agreement include:

- Definitions: These are important terms that explain factors like the company, affiliate application, website, affiliate (you), affiliate program, parties, and any other factors that may be relevant to the affiliate program.

- Partnership nature: This section will include what the relationship will be between the affiliate and the company.

- Responsibilities: This section explains what is expected from the affiliate once they join the program. These include the links they use, the products and services they will be promoting, and how to comply with the FTC guidelines.

- Compensation: This section will tell you everything about the profits you will make from every sale, click, or lead you to send to the company. It should also state the payment frequency and any other information relevant to the affiliate.

- Termination: In this section, you will find everything relevant to the termination of your affiliate relationship with the company, including the things you are and are not allowed to do while affiliated. It might also include a term of your contract that is established by the company.

- Confidentiality: This is a non-disclosure section located on the agreement stipulating what information you may share with your audience and what is considered confidential.

- Intellectual property: Who the information belongs to can be found in this section. This might stipulate that any promotional material supplied by the company is the property of the company.

- Warranties: This section talks about any licenses the company or affiliate needs in order to comply with regulations.

Notice: The information supplied above is merely a guideline and should not be considered legal advice. Agreements might vary depending on the affiliate program and companies you are affiliated with.

Comprehending Privacy Policies: There are a few things you need to keep in mind when you create your privacy policy:

- It needs to be easy to read and understand.

- If you create a link to your privacy policy, it needs to be in a place where your audience can easily access it. The optimal position is in the header of your platform.

- A privacy policy must contain the rights your audience has and how they should protect it.

- You should tell your audience whether you are receiving commissions from the links you promote.

- You should add any information about cookies you use on your website.

Adhering to the Federal Trade Commission (FTC) Guidelines: The following guidelines related to affiliate marketing should be followed strictly in order to remain compliant in the industry:

- Ensure you disclose your relationship with the affiliate program without using hard-to-understand language.

- Before adding a link to your content, provide your audience with a disclosure.

- The links you add are not a replacement for your disclosure.

- Hashtags are not acceptable.

- The disclosure you add to a certain link should be placed close to the link so your audience can clearly see it.

- You are allowed to use hyperlinks for your disclosures if they are located on another website.

Ensuring compliance with the General Data Protection Regulation (GDPR): You need to make sure the company offering the affiliate program is complying with these regulations. Some of the things you need to make sure of include:

- Do they have a Data Protection Officer?

- Are they up to date with the new GDRD regulations? I suggest you educate yourself on these regulations so you know what to look out for.

- Do they do a regular information audit?

- Do they process data lawfully?

- What are their implementation processes?

- Does the company keep a record of documentation related to the data they collect?

- Do they offer training on their products and services?

Remembering these four pillars ensures smooth sailing amidst turbulent tides within the regulatory waters surrounding online businesses.

It has been proven that over half of US-based small businesses faced regulatory issues related to their websites' TOS agreements during 2020 alone, signaling an increasing emphasis on proper understanding and implementation regarding these matters!

Sound Knowledge

Sound knowledge about the legal aspects of online businesses propels growth while mitigating risk factors.

Action Steps:

1. Familiarize yourself with TOS agreement basics.

2. Create or update the privacy policy, keeping user interests paramount.

3. Ensure complete adherence to FTC guidelines, especially regarding endorsement disclosures.

4. Understanding the implications of non-compliance vis-à-vis GDPR rules, irrespective of whether they are directly applicable or otherwise to your business model.

5. Consider seeking professional advice to simplify the complexities associated with it.

Remember, one misstep could lead down a rabbit hole, causing unwanted complications; therefore, tread carefully! Happy Navigating!

Chapter 10:

Using Different Platforms

Don't rely on one traffic source and one affiliate program... branch out. –Linxtro

As the above quote says, you need to increase your reach if you want to be successful in the affiliate marketing world. Getting associated with various affiliate programs and using various platforms to promote your products will increase your chances of getting seen and making a profit.

You might be focusing on the existing platforms you are already using, but there are various platforms available for you to use. Below are the seven most popular platforms you can use:

Blog

Creating a blog is possibly the easiest method of creating an affiliate business. However, you need to keep in mind that starting and maintaining a blog takes time and patience, as you would first need to grow your audience before you can start making money. Some of the topics you are able to cover in your blog include:

- Product reviews

- How to guides

- Testimonials on products

- Posts related to the use of the products you advertise

When creating your blog, you need to keep the quality of the content you are creating in mind so you can provide your audience with the valuable information they are looking for. Once you have a good number of followers, you have the ability to monetize your blog through your affiliate marketing programs.

Social Media

This platform is the most obvious of all of the platforms I will be mentioning in this chapter since it is the most used by affiliate marketers. Social media can be used to promote your website, blog posts, or affiliate links. The most popular social media platforms are:

- Twitter
- Facebook
- Instagram
- TikTok
- LinkedIn

You can use different content in your social media posts, like infographics, short videos, and various others. Providing your followers with information they want to see will get you more clicks on your affiliate links, website pages, and social media posts.

YouTube

YouTubers are often affiliated with various programs and this is how they increase the revenue they make through the videos they post. They often recommend products they personally use so their viewers and subscribers can see them and then make a purchase using the affiliate link they put in the description box. From personal experience, I have seen various YouTubers who have signed up with the Amazon affiliate program and they recommend the products they use to everyone who clicks on their video.

One thing you need to remember when advertising your affiliate links on YouTube is that you need to make sure they are relevant to your audience. For example, if your YouTube channel is based around cleaning videos, then adding affiliate links to cleaning products or cleaning appliances will bring you more clicks on your links.

You are also able to create videos that provide your audience with product reviews, how-to guides, or new products. The types of videos you make will depend on what you want to show your audience and the information you want to give them. Remember to keep the content you create as valuable as possible so your viewers will continue to come back to your channel. If they feel you are trying to solve their problems, the likelihood of them subscribing increases significantly.

Niche Website

When creating a niche website, you are creating content that is focused on a specific type of audience. Your website could be related to business, pets, health, fashion, gardening, relationships, food, technology, or any other topic you think your audience might be interested in.

Below are a few steps you can follow to get your niche website set up and ready for your audience:

- Choose your niche

- Search for the right keywords

- Build your website

- Write content that is high-quality and relevant

- Create backlinks your audience will be interested in

- Practice website analysis
- Adjust as needed

The nice thing about creating a niche website is that you can attract a good amount of traffic by focusing all your energy on one niche. You will be surprised to know the number of people who are interested in different topics, and the possibilities are endless.

Podcast

Podcasting has seen a major spike in popularity over the past few years, with more and more people turning to recorded information as opposed to written content. This is because people have become busier than ever, but this doesn't mean that their need to find information has decreased. You are able to turn your podcast into a profitable affiliate business by recommending products to your listeners.

Below are the most popular platforms for creating your podcast:

- Podbean
- Fusebox
- Buzzsprout

Keep in mind that you still need to build your podcast audience before you start promoting your affiliate links to your listeners.

Email Marketing

This was talked about in a previous chapter, but I would like to remind you of the power of email marketing in the affiliate marketing industry. You can create a newsletter to send to the emails you collect through your website sign-up or through your social media popups. Below are the steps to using email marketing in your affiliate business:

- Create informative, downloadable content for your audience

- Collect your audience email IDs

- Create a marketing strategy

- Create a weekly/monthly newsletter to send to your audience.

- Ensure your newsletter contains product recommendations and share them with your audience.

You can pack your newsletter with tons of information on the product recommendations you make and add product reviews, deals, listicles, and any other offers you might find valuable. Should your audience find your content valuable, they will be more likely to make a purchase, and you can make a profit. Keep in mind that creating newsletters for your audience might take a significant amount of work to get right, but you can make a profit from it.

Digital Products

Selling digital products has also increased in popularity over the past couple of years. And the plus side is that you will be able to increase your earnings even more. The way you do this is by selling your digital products while adding affiliate links on your website, and if your audience chooses to do both, you get double earnings. You have the option to sell your digital products on your social media platforms, website, or the following platforms:

- Podia

- Gumroad

- Systeme.io

Some of the digital products you can offer your clients include ebooks, templates, or PDF files, depending on the type of content you are providing your audience with. Keep in mind that you need to add the right affiliate links to your digital products to make them as profitable as possible.

Conclusion

Creating a blog is possibly the first and only thought that comes to the minds of various affiliate marketers, but the reality is that affiliate marketing is not just restricted to writing blog posts. You have an array of options to increase your profitability. The platforms mentioned above are just the tip of the iceberg; there are various others, but these are just the most profitable at the moment.

Use the information I provided you with above and start making money with your affiliate marketing business today!

Chapter 11:

Mistakes to Avoid

I would say that the biggest mistake that people make in affiliate marketing is not doing their homework before they get started. –Shawn Collins

Affiliate marketing might seem very straightforward to accomplish and make a significant amount of money if done right, but in reality, even successful marketers still need to be careful of mistakes and how to avoid them. Making mistakes is human, but making the wrong mistakes could be damaging to your brand and your reputation. Below are some of the most common mistakes you should avoid if you want to become successful in your affiliate marketing business.

Not Helping, Just Selling

Developing a mindset of only getting sales is possibly the first mistake you can make as an affiliate marketer. It often leads to less-than-fabulous content and does not give the desired results. Your first and most important thing to focus on should be creating content that readers find valuable. Put your readers first and show them the benefits of the products you are promoting instead of focusing on the features.

Avoid causing friction with your readers as much as possible. Place banner ads where they need to be without frustrating your visitors. You should also consider whether your pop-ups will be considered intrusive by Google. Every banner ad and notification request has its own set of consequences, and it's your job to determine whether they are worth the friction.

Producing Low-Quality Content

As an affiliate marketer, your content is your product. The more clicks you get on your website, the more assured you can be that readers will find your content valuable. Remember that one great post will far outweigh the strength of 10 okay posts. There are a few steps you need to follow if you want to ensure that your posts outrank those of your competitors. You should first determine if your topic is feasible. Once you have done that, you can go ahead and do some keyword research to uncover what you should do to outrank the competition.

Answer the following questions as truthfully as possible:

Do you need more root domain backlinks: MozBar can be used to establish how many backlinks your competitors have.

How many words should your posts contain? You should aim for at least 1,800 words on your first page. This should be a general guideline for all your content.

Are you adding images to your posts? Images are proven to attract more readers than posts without them. You should also take the readability of your posts into consideration.

These answers will help you come up with top-ranking content for your blog or website. Once you have written your content, you need to put in as much effort as possible into promoting it as possible. You can do this by:

- Sharing your link on social media
- Sending it to an email list
- Ask fellow bloggers to add a link to your guide on their websites.

Ignoring Site Speed

If your website takes longer than two seconds to load, then the chances of readers leaving your site increase by 50%. Users are often impatient and don't want to wait to get the information they are looking for. You can use a site like GTMetrix.com to establish what is causing your site to load slowly. Some of the common causes of slower site speed are server response times, larger files, or the method by which content is delivered.

Your site might not be able to load within two seconds, but adding plugins can help you improve this. The time you spend implementing the actions to improve your site speed will help improve your user experience and increase your rankings and conversion rates.

Ignoring Readability

As the ages have evolved, readers are no longer interested in hard-to-read or extensive content; they are looking for quick information. You should avoid using fonts that are smaller than 16 pt., especially when you are attempting to attract mobile users. Line height, fonts, and blog templates are a few of the other things you should keep in mind when writing your blogs. Serif font is the best option when it comes to blog posts and paragraph text.

Avoid writing long sentences or paragraphs, as it will make it difficult for individuals to read, and they will quickly lose interest. Paragraphs should also be kept to four sentences or less. The words you use are another important consideration because if you need to look up the spelling of a word you want to write, then it would be best to leave it out. Keep your posts at a seven- or eighth-grade level to hold the attention of readers.

Not Understanding the Product You're Selling

You need to invest time in learning everything you can about the product you are writing about. Don't think that readers aren't savvy. Readers are willing to question everything you are telling them, especially when they are unsure of what you are trying to tell them. You can improve on this by subscribing to blogs like Quora or Reddit so you can look up common questions your readers might be asking. Do as much research as you can so you can build readers' trust and engagement.

Ignoring SEO

Utilizing SEO when composing a new post is possibly one of the most important things you should do when trying to gain readers. You should include proper title tags and meta descriptions to help your content come up in search results. When you're not using the right keywords for your content, you might make it impossible for readers to find it.

Do some research on a title tag and meta description that will compel readers. You should look at this as a sales pitch so it's worth it to take your time. The more readers can relate to your title, the higher the chances they will click through your page. You should also focus on links and external links because they help you establish an information hierarchy. External links will help you indicate the credibility of the third party's site.

Before publishing your post, take another quick read through your content and see where you are able to add a few more links.

Not Understanding Your Audience

Not knowing your audience and what their needs are is possibly one of the biggest mistakes any affiliate marketer can make. Whether you are new to affiliate marketing or have done it for a long time, it's important to get to know your target market. You will not be able to create content that solves problems if you are unaware of the problems, would you? Take the time to do some research on what your audience is looking for before starting your affiliate marketing business.

Take the time to create marketing personas for your audience using the research and insights you have collected. Doing this will give you an idea of who is looking for your products and who you should market them to. You will also be able to adjust your content to suit the needs of your audience, which will give you an advantage in the industry. You are also able to conduct surveys to get a better understanding of your audience and what their needs are.

Not Doing Research

Conducting the necessary research before starting your affiliate business is possibly the most important step you should take. It might seem like a daunting task, but it can mean the difference between success and failure. Some of the things you need to research when starting an affiliate marketing business include:

- Niches
- Affiliate programs
- Audiences
- Keywords
- SEO topics

- Marketing forms
- Content

Understanding and incorporating this information into your affiliate marketing business will give you an advantage in the industry and help you scale your business.

Not Building a Platform

It might seem daunting to create a website for your affiliate marketing business but rest assured; it is completely necessary. With technological advances, it has also never been easier to create a website that is both functional and attractive to your users. Of course, you can only use social media, paid ads, emails, and forums to advertise your affiliate business, but this takes a significant amount of time and effort to generate enough traffic to make a profit.

You can have a piece of self-managed online real estate by creating your own affiliate website. It will also give you a head start in your business. Another benefit of having your own website is that you won't need to go looking for traffic; it will come to you. A website removes any limitations on building profits and can help you generate daily commissions. Once your website has increased in popularity, you also have the ability to sell it for more than 30 times its worth.

Choosing the Wrong Niche

Simply choosing a niche you are not passionate about could be damaging to your affiliate marketing business. You shouldn't just look at the potential profits you can make within a niche; you need to choose a niche you want to create content for, because this will motivate you to continue. You should also avoid picking a niche that has too much competition because it could mean that you won't have a large enough audience.

Picking a niche that you are passionate about will prevent you from getting bored. You should also ensure the niche you choose is popular, so you can ensure a significant amount of clicks on your website. You should also check the profitability of your niche to ensure you will be making a profit from your affiliate efforts.

Writing Unprofitable Product Reviews

When writing product reviews, you need to ensure they will convert into sales and it doesn't sound like a sales pitch. Some of the mistakes you need to avoid when writing product reviews include:

- Generic information: People who go looking for product reviews are looking for honest personal experiences and not just another AI-generated opinion. When writing product reviews, you need to be as honest as possible. It's okay to have an opinion.

- Not showing yourself: Show how you are using the product you are reviewing as much as possible. Avoid telling your audience about your experience; they want to see it.

- Not having a call-to-action: Adding a call-to-action button to your product reviews will help increase your conversion rates because your audience will be more likely to click on your links.

- Being too positive: When writing product reviews, you need to add both the pros and cons related to it. This is because there is no such thing as a perfect product and everything has a con. Doing this will increase the trust and reliability your audience has in you.

- Emphasizing the benefits: Only focusing on the features of the product you are reviewing can be a big mistake. This is because the website you are referring your audience to already has all the feature information your audience needs. Instead, you need to focus on the benefits the products have and which of their problems they can help solve.

Not Organizing Your Workflow

When starting an affiliate marketing business, you need to know that you are your own boss and that no one will be standing behind you telling you what you need to do next. An affiliate marketing business should be run like any other business. You need to have intentions behind everything you do. In order to organize your workflow, you can follow the tips below:

- Create a work schedule
- Batch similar tasks together
- Create a to-do list every night
- Create a designated workspace
- Start with your most important task first
- Remove any distractions, including your phone

Do some research on tools that will help you organize your day.

Not Staying True to Yourself

Staying true to yourself means you need to promote products you are passionate about, not just products that promise these wonderful things without actually delivering on their promise. You can choose to promote high-quality products that deliver results, which sounds like a much better option, doesn't it?

Stick to products you believe in, and don't stretch yourself so thin that you lose sight of what actually matters. Be as honest with yourself and your audience as possible because this will help you build trust and reliability. Your first priority should be to put your audience first.

Getting Impatient

Letting your doubts get the better of you is possibly the worst mistake you can ever make with your affiliate marketing business. The affiliate marketing success stories you read online didn't happen overnight and took a couple of months, even years, to achieve. You need to be willing to put in as much spare time as possible to create content for your audience. Your hard work will start to pay off soon enough.

The key is to never lose faith and push through. Affiliate marketing is not a get-rich-quick scheme, and it takes a significant amount of hard work and dedication to get right.

Chapter 12:

Case Study Corner

In the long run, your character will decide your ultimate success more than anything else. –Ray Croc.

As you embark on your journey into the world of affiliate marketing, it's essential to understand that this isn't a get-rich-quick scheme. This business model requires hard work, dedication, and most importantly, ethics.

Affiliate marketing is an incredible opportunity to generate income by promoting other people's products or services. However, like any business endeavor, it has its own successes and failures. Believe it or not, the difference often boils down to one key factor: ethics.

In the online world, where trust is fragile and easily broken, ethical practices have become more important than ever before. Successful affiliate marketers understand this principle; their success depends on selling products and building lasting relationships based on trust and respect.

Now, let's dive into some real-world examples of how ethics can impact your success in affiliate marketing.

Ethics Can Make or Break Your Business

If there's one thing we've learned from years of observing successful affiliates, it's that ethical behavior pays off in the long run. You build strong foundations for sustainable growth when you prioritize honesty over quick profits and treat customers with respect rather than seeing them as mere dollar signs.

Research supports this observation too! According to the Nielsen Global Trust in Advertising report (2015), 83% of consumers say they completely or somewhat trust recommendations from friends and family while purchasing online. So, when you promote a product honestly without exaggerating its benefits or hiding its flaws, you're likely to win customer loyalty, which means more recommendations!

Let's look at Pat Flynn, for example; he's an incredibly successful affiliate marketer who puts ethics first. He always discloses his affiliates openly and honestly reviews products, including their pros and cons, which has earned him immense trust amongst his audience, leading to phenomenal success.

However, not all stories end so successfully...

Remember 'The Rich Jerk'? His flashy site promised easy riches through affiliate marketing but lacked transparency about what exactly was being sold, leading many unsuspecting individuals to lose money instead of making it. It wasn't long before his unethical practices caught up with him, resulting in a loss of credibility amongst potential buyers and eventually causing his downfall eventually.

Integrity is doing the right thing even when no one is watching. –C.S Lewis.

Analysis shows us that adopting ethical practices like transparency about affiliations and honest product reviews results in long-term profitability, whereas dishonesty may lead to short-term gains but eventually failure due to a loss of consumer trust.

Case studies from scientific research papers reveal similar conclusions:

A University of Illinois (n.d.) study found that businesses that upheld strict ethical standards outperformed rivals financially, proving a link between ethics and success. Facts and statistics back these claims further: The Edelman Trust Barometer (2019) reported that 81% of consumers need to be able to 'trust the brand' before purchasing!

Success Stories

To give you an idea of how successful you can be with your affiliate marketing business if you follow all the tips and tricks contained in this book, here are some success stories of real-life affiliate marketers.

Darran Rowse

Darren Rowse is the owner of ProBlogger.net. He is possibly one of the most influential bloggers in the industry today. He is always open to sharing his success, the techniques he uses, and the history of how he started. He has been able to earn almost half a million dollars in revenue from Amazon's affiliate marketing program. Darren started his affiliate journey in 2003 and only started earning a sustainable commission in 2008, so you can say he is the perfect example of how long it might take to get successful in the industry.

Darren has created and maintains various websites built with the purpose of helping others build and maintain their own affiliate marketing businesses. Darren enjoys discussing why he has chosen Amazon as the affiliate program to join, and he has the following points to support his choice:

- Amazon is a trusted company in e-commerce and has a number of verified affiliates already on its panel.

- Your audience only has to click on one of your links, and it works for any product they choose to purchase since the link is directly related to your Amazon affiliate profile. This means that even if you refer someone to a $5 book and your audience decides to purchase a TV worth $500, you will get a commission on the TV.

- Amazon provides their affiliates with a ton of tools they can use to promote their products to their audience. You can also get various short links to use on your platform to promote products to your audience.

- Amazon has various products available for you to promote, but there are very few products they don't have available on their platform.

David McSweeny

David is the owner and creator of Top5SEO.co.uk. He has been in the industry for 15 years and is considered to be an SEO expert. David has increased his income from $0 to $4,000 a month in only six months with the tips and tricks he shares with various other potential affiliate marketers.

In the posts he shares with others, he explains how he spent the first month of his affiliate journey simply creating and setting up his platform and choosing the right products for his business. He talks about the amount of research he had to do in order to become successful. David writes reviews of the various products he promotes to his audience and aims for around 2,500 words per post. He started with only 800 visitors when he launched his site and made a mere $115.

During his second month of affiliate marketing, David's visitors increased to 2,200, and he made $391. He goes on to say that he spent around 234 hours during the first four months of his affiliate business.

This is Why I'm Broke

The website *www.thisiswhyimbroke.com* has grown significantly in a matter of a few years. This website sells anything you can think of, from color-changing showerheads to drones, pajamas, and even a magic wand TV remote. The website has made around $20,000 a month through the Amazon affiliate program. This website has also teamed up with sites like eBay, partner sales and referrals, ThinkGeek, and Wicked Lasers.

The owner of this website struggled to build his website when he just started. But since then, he has created the right formula to reach success, which includes adding infinite scrolling, carefully selected products, and carefully picked images. This site also teaches its audience how to recreate its success. This site remains lucrative and has more than one million visitors on a yearly basis.

Chris Guthrie

Chris is the creator of UpFuel. Upfuel provides Chris with an annual revenue of upwards of $45,000, which could have been doubled if he hadn't sold one of his other lucrative websites. Chris has also created a post teaching others how to start their own affiliate marketing business. Below is a summary of the tips Chris gives his audience:

- Pick a good niche: Your niche is possibly the most important part of your affiliate marketing business. Your niche needs to speak to your audience if you want to earn an income from your business.

- Avoid Amazon boxes, sidebars, or tables: Go for content links when creating your platform since they are more attractive and will increase the number of clicks you receive from your audience. Do not mislead your audience by promoting one thing and then having your link take them to Amazon.

- Convert your links into clickable images: Images are often more attractive than word links. So consider changing your affiliate links into attractive images. When doing this, ensure that your image takes your audience to the relevant site and not just to an image.

- Link to Amazon frequently: Avoid adding too many links to your content, as this could result in a penalty incurred by Google. Chris recommends that you stick to between five and ten links per post. This recommendation is dependent on the length of your content, so it requires you to do some trial and error to see where your threshold is for incurring a penalty.

- Write genuine reviews: Reviews have been proven to have the highest conversion rate. You can enlist others to help you with this.

- Cover the holidays: Utilizing holiday and Black Friday promotions can help you increase your profits significantly since they are in high demand for viewers.

- Expand your niche: As your platform grows and you gain more followers and clicks, you can expand on your niche and add more products to your portfolio. If you are selling makeup, then you can expand to jewelry, clothing, and shoes. Just ensure that you are not joining too many affiliate programs at once and that the products you choose add value to your audience.

- Promote cheaper products at the beginning of the month and expensive ones at the end: It's a fact that you would rather capitalize on the 8% commission that Amazon offers as opposed to 4%, but you need to vary the commission rates you receive through your affiliate business.

- Evergreen content: Add as much evergreen content to the content you create as possible. Evergreen content should be updated regularly and you need to inform your audience that you are providing them with the most relevant information.

As you can see, there are various affiliates that have been able to make a success out of their affiliate businesses. If you are not convinced after reading these success stories, then you might want to do some more research online on successful affiliate marketers. There are a ton of success stories for you to indulge in.

Conclusion

So here are some action steps:

1. Begin with clear disclosure about your affiliations
2. Resist the temptation to oversell goods or services

3. Be as transparent as possible regarding the benefits and drawbacks each product or service recommend

By putting these into practice, along with lessons learned from past case studies, you're well on your way to becoming the next big success story in ethical affiliate marketing!

Chapter 13:

Final Thoughts

Online marketing isn't about hitting some home runs; it's about base hits over the long term. –Ken Evoy

In the immortal words of Albert Einstein, "I never think of the future. It comes soon enough." Yet here we are, on a quest to understand what lies ahead for ethical affiliate marketing. For those unfamiliar with this term, it is a type of performance-based marketing that rewards affiliates for each visitor or customer brought by their own marketing efforts.

The Future of Affiliate Marketing

Imagine sailing in an ocean called "The Internet," and your ship is called 'Affiliate Marketing.' You have an ethical compass guiding your way through choppy waters. Now, picture the horizon. That's where we're headed—the future.

Let's begin our journey with predictions based on current trends...

Predictions Based on Current Trends

The first ray of dawn indicates increased transparency. As more people become internet savvy, they demand openness from marketers about their relationships with brands. This trend not only builds trust but also fosters loyalty among customers.

Next up: personalization. Just like how Netflix suggests movies based on your history, affiliate marketers can use data to offer personalized experiences. No more one-size-fits-all approach; in the future, every click counts, and every user matters.

Lastly, let's talk about automation—our friendly robot overlords aren't taking over yet! However, tools that automate routine tasks are becoming increasingly popular in affiliate marketing. These time-saving marvels allow markers to focus on strategy and creativity instead.

Key Idea: The future promises greater transparency, personalized content, and efficient automation tools for affiliate marketers!

Staying Ahead in a Rapidly Evolving Industry

It's no secret that staying ahead in the fast-paced world of digital marketing feels like running on a treadmill set at max speed while juggling flaming swords (Don't try this at home!)

Don't just follow trends blindly; question them critically before jumping aboard any bandwagons. Remember: Not all shiny objects are gold!

Moreover, embrace change as a constant companion rather than a disruptive foe. Adaptability is key when navigating this ever-changing landscape.

Another proven way of staying ahead with affiliate marketing is to make use of AI tools to help you generate content that is both informative and valuable to your audience. AI is the future of most businesses, but even more so in the world of affiliate marketing. Educate yourself about this revolutionary trend and start getting ahead of your competition by making use of the most valuable tool available right now.

Finally, nurture creativity within yourself and your team because unique ideas stand out amidst internet noise, like neon signs against a dark sky.

Continuing Education Resources for Staying Up-to-Speed

Education is lifelong; even seasoned sailors need updated maps to chart their course accurately! Here are some resources:

Blogs: Subscribe to industry-leading blogs such as Affilorama or Authority Hacker.

Online Courses: Websites like Udemy offer comprehensive courses tailored for different knowledge levels.

Podcasts: Tune into podcasts such as 'The Affiliate Guy' during commutes or workouts.

Networking Events or Webinars: They provide opportunities for learning directly from successful peers!

Remember Winston Churchill's advice? "To improve is to change; to be perfect is to change often."

If things seem challenging now, remember there was once a time when simple tasks seemed daunting too! If you find yourself struggling with advanced techniques or if challenges seem insurmountable, consider seeking help from mentors or professional agencies specializing in affiliate marketing strategies.

As we sail towards unknown horizons, remember why problems occur. They exist, so solutions can be found! And who is better than you, equipped with knowledge and resolve to steer towards success?

To wrap things up:

- Be transparent and personalize
- Don't fear robots—automate!
- Question trends
- Embrace change

- Nurture creativity
- Never stop learning

As we conclude this chapter, keep pondering what Albert Einstein said about thinking of the future. He didn't do it because it came soon enough. But armed with these insights, hopefully, when it does arrive, you'll be ready!

Getting Started with Affiliate Marketing

If you don't find a way to make money in your sleep, you'll work until you die. –
Warren Buffet

There is no doubt that building a successful affiliate marketing business takes time and hard work, but how exactly should you get started? Anyone can start their own online business; it doesn't matter where you are from, what type of education you have, or if you have a certain skill set. It might be one of the smartest moves you ever make when you decide to get started with affiliate marketing, so I would like to help you on this journey.

Below are four easy steps to help you on this exciting journey to financial freedom.

1. Choose Your Topic or Niche: When you start your affiliate marketing business, you should ensure you are starting with a topic you enjoy. If you love cooking, then you might want to start a website where you write recipes or inform your viewers of tips and tricks to improve your cooking. You can then start looking for affiliate programs in the cooking industry to start monitoring your business.

2. The one thing you need to consider when choosing your topic or niche is whether there are enough people who are interested in it. This means that there should be a market for what you are planning to offer your audience; otherwise, you might find

yourself failing before you get started. Research is your best friend in the affiliate marketing industry, so make sure you do enough of it to get yourself educated for this journey ahead. This topic was covered in more detail in Chapter 4.

3. Build Your Website: Now that you have your topic or niche in mind, it's time to start planning your website or platform. Your website is the window to your business, and building a great one is the foundation you need if you want to scale your business in the future. This point was explained in detail in Chapter 6.

4. Find Affiliate Programs: More and more companies are offering affiliate programs to individuals who are looking to promote their products or services while earning an income. Once again, research is your best friend here. Finding an affiliate program that suits both your niche and your needs simply requires you to go scouring the internet. Finding the right affiliate programs was covered in Chapter 5.

5. Earn Commission: Earning commission with an affiliate program is easy and straightforward. All you have to do is advertise your links, and as soon as someone clicks on them and makes a purchase, you earn a commission.

Final Thoughts

The secret to change is to focus all your energy not on fighting the old but on building the new. —Socrates

An affiliate marketer's journey is akin to a tree's life cycle. The seed, your core idea, is a planet in the fertile soil of the market. It sprouts into a sapling, gaining strength over time with the right nourishment. Relevant content and trustworthy relationships. But as it grows taller towards the sky, it faces stronger winds and storms, ever-changing market trends, competition, and ethical dilemmas.

Just like how trees change their growth strategies based on their environment but stay true to their nature, as an affiliate marketer, your tactics may evolve with changing circumstances, but your integrity should remain unshaken.

Albert Einstein once said, "Whoever is careless with the truth in small matters cannot be trusted with important things." This applies perfectly to affiliate marketers. Your readers trust you for authentic reviews and advice; misleading them for short-term gains can permanently tarnish your reputation.

Let's delve into maintaining an ethical approach amidst changing circumstances:

- Transparency is Key: Always disclose your affiliations clearly before promoting products or services. Honesty will solidify trust among audiences.

- Prioritize Quality Over Quantity: Promote only products you have used or believe in.

- Respect Privacy: Do not misuse personal data collected from subscribers for unethical practices.

- Continuous Learning: Stay updated about the latest FTC affiliate marketing guidelines.

If trouble brews stronger than anticipated—say a product you promoted turns out defective—apologize sincerely and take corrective measures immediately.

Breakout Box

Key idea: Growing as an affiliate marketer involves mastering new strategies while maintaining constant honesty and transparency.

Now let's turn to some inspiring stories from successful yet ethical marketers.

Jane has been running a fitness blog for five years now. She promotes only organic supplements through her platform after trying them personally. Despite numerous lucrative offers from synthetic supplement manufacturers, Jane has always prioritized her readers' health over monetary gains.

Another example is Mike, who runs a tech review channel on YouTube. He recently found out that one of his affiliates was selling refurbished items as new ones without informing customers about it. Instead of ignoring this issue to avoid losing commission money, he cut ties with them immediately, announcing his decision publicly.

These stories confirm that staying honest might seem challenging initially but eventually leads to sustainable success by creating a loyal customer base.

As we reach the end of our journey through this book, here are some practical next steps:

- Review all existing promotional content on your platform, ensuring clear disclosure.
- Evaluate all products and services being promoted currently using an ethical lens.
- Plan regular updates regarding FTC guidelines.

Remember, there's no shortcut to lasting success. True victory lies in reaching the destination and enjoying the journey ethically.

To wrap up, here are some key takeaways:

- Transparency fosters trust, which leads to sustained growth.
- Quality over quantity ensures long-term success.
- Respecting privacy builds credibility.

- Continuous learning keeps one updated and adaptable.

As we close this chapter, remember what Winston Churchill said: "Success isn't final; failure isn't fatal; it's courage that counts." So muster up the courage and step forth fearlessly, keeping ethics intact. After all, growing tall while rooted firmly within principles makes one truly unstoppable!

Conclusion

The beauty of affiliate marketing is that it's a win-win situation for everyone involved. –Pat Flynn

Welcome to the final section of this book. I would like to give you a breakdown of all the information you received throughout this book so you can easily find it in case you need to refresh your memory.

Chapter 1: What affiliate marketing is and what it involves was discussed in the very first section of this book. The ecosystem of affiliate marketing and why it is important to remember were also discussed in this chapter.

Chapter 2: Using internet marketing to build your affiliate marketing business can yield great success. This chapter discusses everything around this topic.

Chapter 3: Picking the right niche for your affiliate marketing business could mean the difference between success and failure. With the tips from this chapter, you can choose a niche wisely. There is a sea of affiliate programs available to choose from, but how do you choose the right one? The second part of this chapter discussed everything you need to know about choosing the right affiliate program for your niche and audience.

Chapter 4: Your platform is the window to your products and services, so you need to build one that resonates with your customers. Refer back to this chapter to refresh on what you need to do to build a successful platform.

Chapter 5: Customers need to trust you if you want them to buy from you now and in the future. That is why it is important to build your reputation, trust, and credibility. Refresh what you learned on this topic by taking another look at the content of this chapter.

Chapter 6: Without traffic to your website, you won't be able to sell any of your products. Ensuring you attract enough visitors to your website can remedy this situation. This chapter gives you all the tips and tricks you need to succeed. Sales funnels are the most important tools for affiliate marketing, and you need to use them correctly if you want to succeed. Take a look at the final section of this chapter if you want to refresh your memory about how to convert visitors into buyers using sales funnels.

Chapter 7: You will come across various affiliate marketing strategies as you build your business. In this chapter, I gave you information on some of the proven strategies you can use to grow your business.

Chapter 8: Being successful with your affiliate marketing business means you need to check up on your performance regularly. If you see that your strategy is not working, you need to be willing to make adjustments. Find out more about how to do this in this chapter. Another important lesson I covered in this chapter was scaling your business to increase your profitability. Review this chapter to refresh your memory on these important topics.

Chapter 9: An overlooked part of affiliate marketing is the legal obligations that come with running your business. This is covered in detail in this chapter, so make sure you refresh your memory and review what you learn so you don't fall into any legal pitfalls.

Chapter 10: Social media has various platforms you can use to grow your affiliate business. In this chapter, I discussed the various platforms and how you can use them to your benefit.

Chapter 11: Even if affiliate marketing seems straightforward, there are still some mistakes you need to be careful of and attempt to avoid. Some of the most important mistakes were discussed in this chapter.

Chapter 12: Reading through case studies is possibly the most effective way of remembering what you learned because you get to read real-life stories. This chapter was written for you with that in mind.

Chapter 13: The future of affiliate marketing is as bright as ever. The reasons why are worth remembering since they will motivate you to continue on your journey. You were told about the reasons in this chapter. Getting started with affiliate marketing can be scary, but with the information contained in this chapter, you have all the tools you need. The final section of this chapter is a summary of my final thoughts on the contents of this book.

Congratulations on reaching the end of this book. I hope you learned everything you need to know about starting your own affiliate marketing business and growing it to its full potential. Please leave a review and rating and leave a comment telling me what you would like to read about next so I can continue to provide you with books containing information you want to read and lessons you want to learn.

Nothing is stopping you now, so go out there and start your affiliate marketing business TODAY!!!!

If you enjoyed reading this book and found it informative, please leave a rating and review to let me know what you thought. Please also feel free to let me know if you have any other topics you would like to read about so I can continue to write informative content for you.

Glossary

Ad Network: A network that connects affiliates with affiliate programs. Ad networks are used to reach various websites at once while increasing the amount of traffic you get.

Advertiser: Advertisers are the companies that are selling products or services. They pay affiliates for any sales made from their links.

Affiliate link: This is a unique code assigned to every marketer to use on their advertising platform in order to generate leads for their affiliate program.

Affiliate program: An agreement entered into by an advertiser and a marketer where a fee is paid for generating clicks, sales, or leads from links provided.

AI (Artificial Intelligence): A computerized tool that makes use of human intelligence but is processed by computer systems. It can also assist with communication, decision-making, and learning.

Backlinks: These are links from other websites that go to the same website you are referring your audience to.

Banner ads: These are ads affiliates use to advertise products from their affiliate programs.

Click-through rate: This rate establishes how many times your audience has clicked on your links instead of just viewing them on your website. This should be checked regularly, especially when you use banner ads on your website.

Click-through: When your audience clicks on your links and goes straight to the website you are recommending.

Commission: This is the compensation you will receive for every sale made through your unique affiliate link.

Conversion rate: Your conversion rate is established by taking the number of times your links have been clicked on and dividing it by the number of times your ads have been viewed, multiplied by 100, and you will get your conversion rate in percentage.

Conversion: Every time your audience makes a purchase through your link, it is considered a conversion. This could be anything from purchasing a product or service to subscribing to a newsletter or completing a form on your affiliate program's website.

Cookies: Cookies are text files sent to website users that assign a specific ID to an individual who clicks on an affiliate link.

CPC-Cost per click: This is when you pay for a specific platform every time someone clicks on one of your ads. It is possibly one of the most cost-effective advertising methods.

CPL-Cost per lead: It is considered a lead when your audience takes action and fills out a form with all the details required by the website.

CPS-Cost per sale: A sale only happens when a purchase is completed, and payment has been made by the person who clicked on your link.

CPV-Cost per view: This advertising method entails that you pay for every time your ad is placed where your audience can see it. You can also easily calculate the earnings you will receive if you have a clear indication of what your revenue is.

Daily budget: This is the maximum budget you are willing to spend on a specific campaign you run for your ads. Descriptions, images, and advertised products are usually paid out of this budget.

Disclosure: A notice you put on the platform you use that informs your audience that you are making a profit from any sale made from your affiliate links. It is of utmost importance for you to add this disclosure so you can remain compliant.

Domain authority: This is a score out of 100 that indicates how you will rank on search engines.

Double opt-in: This happens after a subscriber has confirmed that they want to join a subscription and they agree to the terms of service.

Duplicate content: This is when you use the same or similar content across various platforms.

Dynamic tracking: This tracking allows you to track the amount you are investing in your advertisements and the activity you are receiving.

EPC (Earnings per click): This is the amount you will receive every time your links get 100 clicks. You can calculate this amount by taking the profit you receive, dividing it by the number of clicks you have received, and then multiplying it by 100. This will give you your earnings per click as a percentage.

First click: This is when your affiliate program rewards the first affiliate to get a click on a specific link.

Inbound link or backlink: A link from any website that is not yours.

Incentivized affiliates: This is when you get incentivized when your audience completes a specific action. The incentive is usually in the form of commission, prizes, discounts, money, or free subscriptions.

Index: An index contains all the websites that come up when an individual searches for something specific. You should always ensure that your website shows up on the index, or it might not be available to your audience.

Keyword density: A direct relationship between the number of keywords you use and the words that actually show up in your content.

Keyword research: The research you use to find the right keywords to use in your content so you can pop up in search engine results.

Keyword: Specific words used to increase the likelihood of getting on search engine results. Using the most relevant keywords for your niche is the key to success.

Link building: The practice of getting various links from other websites and adding them to your own.

Loyalty affiliates: This is similar to a commission-based affiliate that gets incentivized for clicks on links. These affiliates often make a long-term commitment to the affiliate program.

Manual approval: This is when an affiliate needs to be approved before being allowed to join an affiliate program. The items that need to be checked before approval include identity status, financial status, address, credit, etc. After these things have been checked, an affiliate can either be approved to join the program or rejected.

Maximum budget: The maximum budget you are willing to spend on running campaigns. Once this budget runs out, your campaign automatically stops.

Meta Description: An element, namely HTML or XHTML, that gives a description of your website to the various search engines.

Mobile affiliates: Affiliates who are looking for an audience that uses their mobile phones and who are looking for products for their mobile phones.

Niche marketing: Affiliates who are looking at a specific niche when starting their affiliate marketing business.

Off-page SEO: These factors have an impact on your website in all of the organic search results. They are off-site because they are not controlled by you or your page. This could include your page rank and the popularity of your links.

On-Page SEO: These factors have an impact on your website in all of the organic search results. It is the opposite of off-page SEO because it is a factor that is controlled by you or the coding on your page. These include your HTML code, keyword placements, meta tags, and the density of the keywords you use.

Opt-in Email: This is the email that is requested by the receiver.

Outbound link: These are links not directly related to your own website link.

Page authority: This is a rank that helps you predict how your page will rank on search engines.

Page rank: This is used by Google to see where you are in search results. It takes both the quality and quantity of the links you add to your page into consideration. It is not the only algorithm used by Google, but it is the most accurate and popular.

Paid search: These models are used by affiliates who only want to pay when their ads are clicked on by their target audience. You might need to bid on keyword sentences that are relevant to your ad.

Pay bump: This is when you receive higher compensation for an order placed by one of your clients.

Payment threshold: A specific amount of commission you need to accumulate before you are able to withdraw your payment.

Payout: The amount of money you will receive for every conversion you receive. This is determined by your affiliate program owner and could be fixed or dynamic.

Plug-in: A smaller app that adds features to a bigger one.

Portal: This term is used to describe a site that should actually be used as a point of entry to another one, even if it is a homepage.

PPC affiliates: These affiliates get paid per click they receive on the link they are advertising. These links take their audience directly to the website of their affiliate program, so their audience can take the necessary steps.

PPC: Pay-per-click. With this advertising model, you only pay when your link has been clicked.

PPL: Pay-per-lead. This advertising model only requires you to pay when you get a lead for your affiliate program.

PPS: Pay-per-sale. This commission only gets paid out once a sale is made.

Profit: The amount of commission you make through your affiliate marketing efforts after paying any expenses you have incurred.

Publisher: This is often another term used to describe an affiliate.

Raw clicks: This is the total number of clicks you receive over a certain period. This number includes clicks made by the same client multiple times.

Referring domain: These are backlinks that take your audience to the site they are actually looking for.

Referring URL: A URL that is given to someone to reach your website.

Return on Investment (ROI): This is the amount you are left over after subtracting your expenses from the commission you have made.

Revenue: The amount of money you have made before subtracting any expenses you have incurred.

RON (Run on Network): This is a type of campaign you can run for your business. You can utilize a Run-on-Network (RON) if you want to target websites from another network.

Root domain: A root domain is the shortest type of domain.

Search engine optimization: In order to use Search-Engine-Optimization (SEO), you need to carefully pick the keywords you use for your content so you can rank on search engines. These keywords should be placed strategically so you can appeal to potential website visitors.

Search engine: Search engines come in the form of web pages, texts, news, images, videos, etc., and you will rank on them when using the right keywords.

Search term: This is the term your target audience uses to search for specific content on search engines. This could include a single word or a complete phrase.

Site map: This includes the drop-down menu you add to your website. Essentially, it's a map that tells your audience where to go when looking for a specific topic on your website.

Social marketers: Social marketers are affiliates who use social media to increase their reach to their target audience.

Split testing: Also referred to as A/B testing. This is when you test two different versions of the content, copy, sales, or ads you have on your website against each other to see which one is performing the best.

Subdomain: This is a certain section of your main domain that you can create to complement your main website.

Super affiliates: These are considered the elite affiliates. They often generate more than 90% of the total profits from affiliate programs.

Targeted marketing: This is similar to niche marketing, which means a specific target market is searched for to advertise your product.

Text link: A link that is associated with an advertiser's website without using an image.

Tracking platform: A platform that allows you to track the activity you have both reliably and simply. They provide you with different filters you can use to analyze the data you are looking at.

Tracking software: This is software that does not belong to you that records and tracks the number of visitors you receive on your site.

Tracking URL: These URLs have a specific code attached to them that tracks the visitors through it.

Traffic: The number of visitors you receive on your website.

Unique clicks: These are clicks that have not been made by existing individuals. This happens every time a new person clicks on one of your links. This means that one person can click on your ad nine times, but only the first one will be recorded as being unique.

Unique user: As mentioned above, a unique user is someone who clicks on your website for the first time. Each click after the initial one won't count.

URL: Uniform Resource Locator. This is the address of your website.

Viral marketing: This is when an individual is encouraged to share a specific link with the people they know so the post can go viral.

Web host: A business that provides storage and services for files and pages.

Webmasters: Someone who is in charge of the content and organization of a specific website. They will also take full responsibility for any technical issues that may arise on the website.

White-hat SEO: White-hat SEO is used to improve search performance. This is used by individuals who respect the terms of service of search engines and won't risk getting banned.

White label: A product that is created by a company and sold without a label with the intention of other companies rebranding the product and selling it as their own. White-label products give marketers the freedom to sell the product as they wish.

About the Author

Steve Murry is an author and ethical affiliate marketer. He is a highly successful entrepreneur and author known for his expertise in ethical affiliate marketing techniques. With over 10 years of experience, Steve has established himself as a trusted authority in the world of online business. A loving husband and father, Steve is married with two children and a lovable dog who often keeps him company during his writing sessions.

Steve believes that a balanced personal life is essential for success in both your professional and personal endeavors. Having made ethical business practices the cornerstone of his career, Steve is passionate about promoting transparency and fairness in the ethical marketing industry. Throughout his book, he aims to empower aspiring entrepreneurs by sharing his proven strategies and insights gained from years of hands-on experience. Steve's writing style is engaging, informative, and backed by real-world examples.

His ability to simplify complex concepts makes his book accessible to readers of all stages of their entrepreneurial journey. With a focus on building long-term relationships rather than quick profits, Steve emphasizes the importance of integrity and trust in business. Beyond his writing, Steve is an active participant in various industry events and online communities. He strongly believes in the power of collaboration and enjoys connecting with like-minded individuals to exchange ideas and inspire others.

Through his work, Steve Murry seeks to inspire individuals to pursue ethical affiliate marketing as a viable and sustainable full-time income source. His book serves as a valuable resource for anyone interested in building a successful online business while adhering to ethical principles.

References

Baker, K. (n.d.). *The Ultimate List of Marketing Quotes for Digital Inspiration*. Blog.hubspot.com. https://blog.hubspot.com/marketing/marketing-quotes

David. (2023, April 3). *The Affiliate Marketing Ecosystem Explained For 2023*. Www.davidruhm.com. https://www.davidruhm.com/affiliate-marketing/affiliate-ecosystem-marketing/

Freund, D. (2023, March 30). *7 Common Mistakes Every Affiliate Marketer Needs to Avoid*. Intergrowth®. https://intergrowth.com/affiliate-marketing/mistakes/

Gasparyan, D. (2023, August 23). *Council Post: How To Build Trust And Credibility In Affiliate Marketing*. Forbes. https://www.forbes.com/sites/forbestechcouncil/2023/08/23/how-to-build-trust-and-credibility-in-affiliate-marketing/?sh=431d25185085

Hareem. (2023, May 30). *What are CTAs in Marketing? Explained with Examples*. ContentStudio Blog. https://blog.contentstudio.io/what-are-ctas-in-marketing/#:~:text=Tips%20for%20creating%20compelling%20and%20effective%20CTAs%20that

Hughes, J. (2019, July 9). *5 Ways to Handle Positive and Negative Feedback About Your Affiliate Program | Easy Affiliate*. Easyaffiliate.com. https://easyaffiliate.com/blog/handle-affiliate-feedback/

Kostelanska, J. (2023, March 17). *8 Tips to Improve the UX of Your Affiliate Website*. Post Affiliate Pro. https://www.postaffiliatepro.com/blog/improve-the-ux-of-your-affiliate-website/

Luyken, R. (2023, October 2). *Top 13 Tips on Email Marketing To Supercharge Your Online Business.* LinkedIn. https://www.linkedin.com/pulse/top-13-tips-email-marketing-supercharge-your-online-business-luyken/

M, M. (2022, August 26). *How to Make an Affiliate Marketing Website in 10 Steps to Ensure Your Business Success.* Hostinger Tutorials. https://www.hostinger.com/tutorials/how-to-make-affiliate-marketing-website#:~:text=How%20to%20Make%20an%20Affiliate%20Marketing%20Website%20in

Mahlaka, R. (2022, January 18). *The private sector's big ethics problem unravels after State Capture report.* Daily Maverick. https://www.dailymaverick.co.za/article/2022-01-18-the-private-sectors-big-ethics-problem-unravels-after-state-capture-report/

Marketing, H. T. A. (2023, January 15). *How to Find Your Niche in Affiliate Marketing 2022.* High Ticket Affiliate Marketing. https://highticketaffiliatemarketing.com/find-your-niche/

Miessner, S. (2016, September 23). *How to Increase Conversion Rates using Customer Psychology.* LiveAdmins. https://www.liveadmins.com/blog/how-to-increase-conversion-rates-using-customer-psychology/#:~:text=How%20to%20Increase%20Conversion%20Rates%20using%20Customer%20Psychology

Miszczak, P. (2021, May 22). *Choosing a Domain Name For Affiliate Marketing [Step By Step Guide].* Businessolution.org. https://businessolution.org/domain-name-for-affiliate-marketing/

Navarro, J.G. (2023, January 6). *Affiliate marketing spending in the United States from 2010 to 2022.* Statista. https://www.statista.com/statistics/693438/affiliate-marketing-spending/

Nguyen, L. (2022, August 29). *What is Brand Transparency and Why It Is important?* Latana.com. https://resources.latana.com/post/brand-transparency/

151 + Best Affiliate Marketing Quotes Get Motivation – 2023. (2023, January 20). Make Affiliate. https://makeaffiliates.com/affiliate-marketing-quotes/#:~:text=Top%20Best%20Affiliate%20Marketing%20Quotes%202023%201%201.

Panwar, A. (2023, May 7). *7 Best Platforms To Promote Affiliate Products [Mostly FREE].* Digital Creative Mind. https://digitalcreativemind.com/platforms-to-promote-affiliate-products/

Parsons, J. (2022, January 17). *5 Success Stories from Affiliate Marketers.* Growtraffic Blog. https://growtraffic.com/blog/2022/01/affiliate-marketing-success-stories

Pay-Per-Click Affiliate Marketing: Why PPC Affiliates Need Better Keyword Tools. (n.d.). WordStream. https://www.wordstream.com/pay-per-click-affiliate

Pay-Per-Sale in Affiliate Marketing: Definition and Examples". (n.d.). Www.growann.com. Retrieved October 2, 2023, from https://www.growann.com/glossary/pay-per-sale#:~:text=Pay-per-sale%20is%20an%20affiliate%20marketing%20model%20wherein%20the

Pecánek, M. M., Michal. (2022, November 15). *How to Do Keyword Optimization for SEO (3 Steps).* SEO Blog by Ahrefs. https://ahrefs.com/blog/keyword-optimization/

Piga, A. (2022, May 12). *Council Post: 4 Ways To Better Understand Your Audience.* Forbes. https://www.forbes.com/sites/forbesagencycouncil/2022/05/12/4-ways-to-better-understand-your-audience/?sh=928e7ff54106

Saleh, K. (August 23). *How To Calculate Conversion Rate For Your Website.* Invesp. https://www.invespcro.com/blog/calculate-conversion-rate/

Sagar. (2020, October 5). *A Guide to Choosing the Right Affiliate Program.* Reseller Club. https://blog.resellerclub.com/guide-to-choosing-the-right-affiliate-program/

Semrush Team. (2023, January 4). *Internet marketing.* Semrush Blog. https://www.semrush.com/blog/internet-marketing/?kw=&cmp=Africa_SRCH_DSA_Blog_EN&label=dsa_pagefeed&Network=g&Device=c&utm_content=665443605021&kwid=dsa-2147915052627&cmpid=18364843126&agpid=154786674841&BU=Core&extid=91738547967&adpos=&gad=1&gclid=CjwKCAjw3oqoBhAjEiwA_UaLtqPC9ME2IaNRpP2KF61554NSCR3tY39MhdlH3yuu2YgyQn5GmRQMfxoCGZsQAvD_BwE

Shopify Staff. (2023a, September 7). *What Is Affiliate Marketing? A 2023 Guide to Getting Started.* Shopify. https://www.shopify.com/za/blog/affiliate-marketing

Shopify Staff. (2023b, September 29). *16 Affiliate Marketing Tips & Strategies to Earn More Money.* Shopify. https://www.shopify.com/blog/affiliate-marketing-tips

Simon. (2022a, July 7). *Top 10 Common Mistakes Every Affiliate Marketer Should Avoid In 2023.* Commission Academy. https://commission.academy/blog/affiliate-marketing-mistakes/

Simon. (2022b, December 1). *How Scalable Is Affiliate Marketing? 12 Things To Know In 2023.* Commission Academy. https://commission.academy/blog/how-scalable-is-affiliate-marketing/#:~:text=How%20Do%20You%20Scale%20Affiliate%20Marketing%3F%201%201.,8%208.%20Target%20Money%20Keywords%20...%20More%20items

Sramek, E. (2021, April 21). *Data analysis tools for affiliate marketing business*. Scaleo. https://www.scaleo.io/blog/data-analysis-tools-for-affiliate-marketing-business/

Sramek, E. (2023, April 13). *9 types of commission models in affiliate marketing*. Scaleo. https://www.scaleo.io/blog/9-types-of-commission-models-in-affiliate-marketing/

The Essential Affiliate Marketing Glossary of Terms (2023 Update). (n.d.). Mobidea Academy. https://www.mobidea.com/academy/affiliate-marketing-glossary/

Top Affiliate Marketing Quotes to Motivate You. (n.d.). SmartScale. Retrieved October 9, 2023, from https://smartscalemarketing.com/affiliate-marketing-quotes/#:~:text=%22Revenue%20is%20king.%20Tying%20your%20content%20to%20revenue

Vora, A. (2023, July 14). *15 Call-to-Action Statistics You Need to Know About to Increase Your Conversion Rate*. HubSpot. https://blog.hubspot.com/marketing/personalized-calls-to-action-convert-better-data

Printed in Great Britain
by Amazon